WITTGENSTEIN'S TRACTATUS
AND THE MODERN ARTS

OTHER WORKS BY JORN K. BRAMANN

Self-Determination: An Anthology of Philosophy and Poetry (ed.)

Capital As Power: A Concise Summary of the Marxist Analysis of Capitalism

Unemployment and Social Values: A Collection of Literary and Philosophical Texts (ed.)

Sunny Side Up: Industrial Strength Poetry

Gainful Unemployment: A Video Meditation After Thoreau

The Water Woman: A Video Drama

TRANSLATIONS

Wolfdietrich Schnurre: *Climb, But Downward,* Poems

Jochen Ziem: *Uprising In East Germany and Other Stories* (with Jeanette Axelrod)

WITTGENSTEIN'S TRACTATUS
AND THE MODERN ARTS

Jorn K. Bramann

ADLER PUBLISHING COMPANY
ROCHESTER, NEW YORK

WITTGENSTEIN'S *TRACTATUS* AND THE MODERN ARTS

By Jorn K. Bramann

First Edition

Copyright © 1985 by Jorn K. Bramann

For information address
Adler Publishing Company
P.O. Box 9342
Rochester, New York, 14604

Cover Design by Sasha Trouslot/Foxglove Graphics

Typographic Systems Analysis by James A. McGrath III

Library of Congress Cataloging in Publication Data

Bramann, Jorn K.
  Wittgenstein's *Tractatus* and the modern arts

  Bibliography: p.
  1. Wittgenstein, Ludwig, 1889-1951. Tractatus logico-philosophicus. 2. Arts, Modern—20th century.
3. Logic, Symbolic and mathematical. 4. Languages—Philosophy. I. Title.
B3376.W563T7322   1985   102   85-1270
ISBN 0-913623-05-9

Acknowledgments will be found at the end of this book

Printed in the United States of America

89 88 87 86 85   5 4 3 2 1

Pour Annette et Yann

CONTENTS

ILLUSTRATIONS

PREFACE

The occasion for writing this book was the preparation of an interdisciplinary M.A. program in Modern Humanities, a program which was to introduce students of various academic backgrounds to the essential features of twentieth century Western Culture. The clarification of the nature of twentieth century art and philosophy had to be a central part of this endeavor.

Due to the interdisciplinary approach of this book, both the philosophy of the *Tractatus* and the peculiar features of Modern Art had to be presented in some detail. Students of arts and letters are usually unacquainted with the works and problems of Analytic Philosophy, and philosophy students often have too limited a grasp of the range and structure of the Modern Arts. In addition, large portions of Wittgenstein's *Tractatus* are so condensed and opaque, and most detailed commentaries so technical, that even philosophers have trouble finding a fruitful access to Wittgenstein's work, let alone students from other fields. The basic features of Wittgenstein's thought and of Modern Art have, therefore, been presented as concretely and nontechnically as possible. No special training in any of the Humanities disciplines is necessary to follow the arguments of this book. The discussions presented here are primarily addressed to readers who seek to inform themselves, not to specialists who are already familiar with the material, and whose major interest is the elaboration of isolated points.

In presenting Wittgenstein's early thought I have not only used its final formulation, the *Tractatus,* but also Wittgenstein's *Notebooks 1914-1916* (the journal from which Wittgenstein extracted most of the material for the final work), and his "Lecture on Ethics" (in which he spelled out in greater detail many of the implications of the condensed statements in the *Tractatus*). Passages from Wittgenstein's personal letters and from reminiscences of his friends have also been used whenever they seemed helpful. The *Tractatus* translation used in most places is that of D.F. Pears and B.F. McGuinness of 1961. In a few places the translation by C.K. Ogden of 1922 seemed preferable, and occasionally I have translated passages myself.

It is impossible to list all the things which went into the writing of this book. Years of undergraduate and graduate training, independent reading, my own attempts at writing, and innumerable informal discussions, have resulted in the ideas of this book. It would be hopeless to even begin searching for the line which separates the insights of others from my own (Particularly inspiring, however, was John Moran's *Toward the World and Wisdom of Wittgenstein's 'Tractatus'*, [See Bibliography]). Nor does finding that line seem particularly important to me. Without presumption I would therefore like to quote on my behalf what Wittgenstein wrote in the Introduction of his *Philosophical Investigations:* "If my remarks do not bear a stamp which marks them as mine, I do not wish to lay any further claim to them as my property."

I want to thank the Philosophy Department and the Administration of Frostburg State College, Maryland, for a sabbatical leave, and the National Endowment for the Humanities for the Fellowships granted to me. Both helped considerably in expediting the completion of this book. Once again, I would like to thank Arthur R. Axelrod for his invaluable editorial advice.

Tucson, Arizona
Fall, 1984

WITTGENSTEIN'S
TRACTATUS
AND THE
MODERN ARTS

INTRODUCTION

The philosophical movement which distinguishes most clearly twentieth century philosophy from earlier schools of thought is Analytic Philosophy (such movements as Existentialism or contemporary Marxism being radicalized continuations of earlier developments), and within Analytic Philosophy, Wittgenstein's *Tractatus Logico-Philosophicus* occupies a most prominent place.[1] A discussion of Wittgenstein's trend-setting work is therefore indispensable for an understanding of twentieth century culture.

In the following chapters the basic contentions of Wittgenstein's *Tractatus* are juxtaposed with those features of the Modern Arts which distinguish twentieth century works from those of earlier art and literary movements. The analysis of Wittgenstein's philosophical doctrines is to elucidate the works of modern artists, writers, and film-makers, and the analysis of modern works of art is to shed light on the basic orientation of modern philosophy. It will hopefully become apparent in this discussion that the experiences and convictions which informed the philosophy of the *Tractatus* are the same as those which dominated the imagination of modern creative artists. This is not to say that the *Tractatus* offers an explicit theory of Modern Art, or that twentieth century artists were concerned about, or even familiar with, the problems of Analytic Philosophy. In fact, Wittgenstein's personal taste in the arts was somewhat conservative and limited to the classical tradition[2], and the philosophical reflections produced by modern artists usually lacked the conceptual precision and sophistication at which modern philosophers aimed. The significant breakthroughs which occurred in twentieth century art and philosophy took place in the mutual isolation which the modern division of labor imposes on industrial as well as intellectual producers. Nevertheless, what Wittgenstein maintained with respect to logic, language, science, ethics, metaphysics, or the structure of reality is closely paralleled by the visions and constructions of modern poems, paintings, buildings, and films. It is basically the same experience of self and world which underlies both areas of expression. It is an experience, furthermore, which will be seen to correspond closely to the social, political and cultural situation as it developed at the beginning of this century.

Before proceeding with this discussion, it will be worth outlining in summary form the nature of Modern Art by enumerating those features that distinguish it from those schools and styles that preceded it, and identifying the main points of Wittgenstein's early philosophy, as contained in the primary theses of his *Tractatus.*

*

The type of art which is referred to as "Modern" was developed rather early in this century (with some of the typical features appearing as early as the last quarter of the nineteenth century). The widespread acceptance of Modern Art, as well as the almost universal use of its peculiar techniques, did not occur until after World War II — a time when the most advanced artists began to suspect that by that time Modernism in the arts had come close to exhausting its genuinely creative possibilities. The decisive breakthroughs of Modern Art, however, have all been achieved during the first two decades of this century, leaving the following generations of modern artists with little more than the refinement of earlier impulses, or the endless repetition of those artistic "revolutions" which became the bread and butter of enterprising publishers and galleries (not to mention the cultural propagandists of the "Free World"). Most of the writers and painters who actually accomplished the early breakthroughs, and who usually risked something by doing so, were born in the 1880s, and they created their most daring work before the outbreak of World War I. It is this time period which also saw the "analytic revolution" in philosophy, and into which falls the conception of those radical ideas which make Wittgenstein's *Tractatus* a landmark of twentieth century thought.

The definition of "Modern Art" is, as that of other historical phenomena, a problem. It seems most adequate, however to think of "Modern Art" as a "family resemblance" concept, i.e., as a concept which comprises a great variety of works of art which do not necessarily have one or several features in common, but which are related to each other by a number of typical features in the way characterized in Wittgenstein's later philosophy:[3] "Modern" are those works of art which do not necessarily have all, but typically most of the following features:

    1. They are ambiguous with respect to the idea of a transcendence, i.e., the idea of transcending the world of mere facts. On the one hand modern authors have severe problems with such metaphysical concepts as a world beyond the world, life after death, a soul without a

body, a Being independent of observable facts, etc. On the other hand the idea of transcending the world of mere facts lingers on, inducing a disposition which relates to the world as something which stands in need of overcoming or redemption.

2. They emphasize the nonrational features of human beings and the world. They appeal to emotions rather than reason, and they are critical of the assumed "Rationalism of Western Civilization," to which they attribute such effects as the mortification of imagination, feeling, and bodily functions.

3. They represent reality as a chaotic conglomerate of fragments, and they prefer forms of representation which approach collages rather than unified, harmonious compositions.

4. They imply a loss of self. While in older works of art one can always uncover an ideal of what a human individual ought to be, twentieth century works tend to promote the "anti-hero," individuals without calling, role-model, community, orientation, or inalienable properties. Modern individuals lack a genuine identity: they either wear a mask, an artificial *persona,* or they profess to be nothing.

5. They undermine all forms of tradition — either directly, by rejecting the past, or indirectly, by using past roles or forms of communication only ironically.

6. They tend to approach the limits of what can be said or imagined. While traditional art forms comprise both the realistic and the fantastic, Modern Art often creates "pictures" of things which cannot even be imagined, thereby destroying the means of art as means of communication. By operating close to the limits of silence, modern painters and writers have become more aware of the limits of their arts than any previous generation of artists.

The list of features given here may not be complete, and the formulation of the points comprising the list could certainly be varied, allowing different emphases, but by and large the features listed above are those which can be found most often in those works which have come to be considered the classics of Modern Art.

*

It is, of course, difficult to give a complete summary of a book which is already extremely condensed. Summaries of the *Tractatus* have always been highly selective, and the present outline is no exception.

Recognition of Wittgenstein's primary theses is guided by the numbering system designed by Wittgenstein himself. Of all the theories and statements of the *Tractatus,* seven theses are distinguished by being numbered 1 through 7. Undoubtedly, Wittgenstein thought that these theses were the major foci of his discussion.

In the following discussion, six of these seven theses well be briefly discussed. Wittgenstein's thesis 6, while of considerable theoretical importance, is too technical to be relevant to the present topic. Thus, certain topics dealt with in the *Tractatus* emerge as primary: the structure of reality, a theory of language, and the nature of logic, and these topics are treated most extensively. Certain other topics do not appear in the list, although they are not necessarily less important: a theory of science, of mathematics, of ethics, of the self, and of the nature of philosophy. They will more or less be ignored in this summary, but most of them are discussed in some detail in the various chapters of this book.

1. *The world is all that is the case.*

Wittgenstein defines reality as the sum total of all facts. By defining reality in this way he excludes the following concepts as illusory: (1) the idea of a transcendence, a world beyond the world of facts; (2) the idea of a realm of "absolute values" which could guide human behavior in a binding way; (3) the idea of a comprehensive ("holistic") order of reality which composes the individual facts into the kinds of system constructed by Aristotle, Hegel, Marx, or other thinkers. Reality, in other words, is a conglomerate of nothing but facts. These facts are without metaphysical meaning ("how things are in the world is a matter of complete indifference for what is higher"[4]), without value ("murder will be on exactly the same level as any other event, for instance the falling of a stone"[5]), and essentially isolated from each other ("one thing can be the case or not be the case, while everything else remains the same"[6]). It is a world which to the thinking individual must appear as profoundly senseless, strange, and incoherent, as the kind of shattered *cosmos* that emerges in the works of modern artists.

2. What is the case — a fact — is the existence of states of affairs.

Facts are not the ultimate constituents of reality, but are further divided into what Bertrand Russell called "atomic facts," and Wittgenstein "states of affairs." The fact that the broom is in the corner, e.g., is composed of the two more elementary facts that the handle is in the corner and the brush is in the corner.[7] And these two facts can be divided into still more elementary ones. "Atomic facts" or "states of affairs" are reached when no further division is possible. Wittgenstein never gave an example of such "states of affairs," but he argued that they must exist: If the division of facts into ever more elementary ones did not ultimately terminate in some "states of affairs," no statement about reality could be made at all.

An "Atomic fact" is still a complex entity. As the non-atomic fact that the broom is in the corner is a configuration of more than one thing, namely a spatial arrangement of broom and corner, so a "state of affairs" is still a configuration of more than one element. To get to the ultimate constituents of reality one has to look at these elements by themselves. They must be absolutely simple, for if they were not, they would be configurations, and thereby complex facts. These absolutely simple elements Wittgenstein called "objects," and together they constitute the "substance" of the world. They are the "substance" because they are always there, and not subject to change. Only the configuration of these atomic particles of the world change. The "substance" of the world is invariant, timeless.

In light of this analysis of reality, the ordinary facts of the world appear as something transient and unstable. Indeed, the world as viewed by the *Tractatus* is on several occasions characterized in accordance with the idea of the *vanitas mundi et fuga saeculi,* the transitoriness of all "worldly" things, that has dominated earlier epoch's quests for religious or metaphysical refuge. The *Tractatus,* to be sure, does not allow for the kind of Christian transcendence in which everything worldly is denounced as vain. Yet, Wittgenstein's quasi-religious devaluation of worldly things is obvious throughout his early writings, and it stands to reason that the *Tractatus'* theory of "substance" carries significant overtones of a religious attitude toward the world.[8]

Wittgenstein's justification of his postulate of a "substance" is not based on metaphysical speculation, but on his analysis of language. Since according to him the essential function of language is to depict reality, every constituent part of language has to correspond to a specific part of the world. As the entirety of language divides into propositions (i.e., descriptive sentences), the world divides into facts. As propositions divide into more elementary propositions, facts divide into "states of affairs." And as elementary propositions divide into "names" (i.e., basic words), states of affairs divide into "objects." "Names" stand for "objects," elementary propositions depict "states of affairs," and propositions depict facts — these are the basic contentions of Wittgenstein's early theory of language. In this way the analysis of language into its constituent parts led to a corresponding analysis of reality, and thus to the postulate of a "substance" that underlies all facts.

3. A logical picture of facts is a thought.

In thinking, one forms pictures of facts. A fact (or a state of affairs) is a configuration of elements. The fact that the book lies on the table, for example, is a certain configuration of book and table. In thinking that the book is on the table one forms some kind of mental picture of this configuration. This mental picture *may* be a simple mental reproduction of the book lying on the table, but it may also be much more abstract. For example, the book may be represented by a red cube and the table by a green one. The image of the red on the green cube may serve as a picture of the above fact. Or, the book may be represented by the letter "a" and the table by the letter "b." Thinking the letter "a" before the letter "b" may picture the fact that the book is on the table. (Thinking the letter "a" *after* the letter "b" may picture that the book is under the table, etc.) Any suitable configuration of any elements in one's mind may serve as a picture of certain facts. A picture need in no way resemble a realistic painting or drawing. Certain graphs in economics, for example, are pictures of facts that are very different from what they depict. Even the grooves in a phonograph record form, in Wittgenstein's sense, a "picture" of a particular piece of music.[9]

When one says that a mental picture is a "logical" one, one means that the configuration of elements represents a *possible* state of affairs. When one thinks that the book is on the table, the book may not actually be there; that is, the picture may be false. But a false picture is still a picture, because it depicts a possible state of affairs. A picture only ceases to be logical when it attempts to represent something which cannot be thought. M.C. Escher's "Belvedere," e.g., displays a "building" which is an impossibility in the strictest sense, for four of the pillars which connect the upper two floors are on both the front *and* the back of the structure. Escher's "Belvedere," in other words, is not a picture in Wittgenstein's sense of the word, because it violates the laws of logic, because it suggests a configuration of elements which is impossible. A genuine thought, by contrast, has to be a possible configuration of elements, it has to be a "logical" picture.

The major significance of Wittgenstein's conception of thoughts as "logical pictures" lies in the implication that thoughts can be not only true or false, but also nonsensical. As Escher's "Belvedere" is not just fantastic in the sense that pictures of green Martians in the streets of New York are fantastic, but strictly unintelligible, so many thoughts (particularly in philosophy and theology) are not merely hard to believe, but literally unthinkable. And, realizing the difference between falseness and nonsensicality, one will not try to refute problematic philosophical and theological contentions by mustering empirical evidence, as would be appropriate in the sciences, but by subjecting the problematic contentions to a rigorous logical analysis to see whether they are logically coherent. One of the major claims of Analytic Philosophy is to have demonstrated that a good many theories of traditional philosophy are neither true nor false, but nonsensical, although at first sight they look like intelligible statements.

4. *A thought is a proposition with sense.*

With this statement Wittgenstein widens his concept of thought as "logical picture" to his "Picture Theory of Language": If a proposition with sense is a thought, and a thought is a logical picture, then a genuine proposition is a logical picture as well. What has to be said about thoughts, also has to be said about the expressions of thoughts, i.e., about language and its central units, propositions. As thoughts, propositions can be not only false (as such statements as "There are oceans on the moon"), but also nonsensical (as such pseudo-statements as "The book lies on the thirteenth century," "The inflation rate is green," or "I see the grin of the Cheshire cat, although I do not see the cat's face or mouth").

To Wittgenstein, the broader implication of his theory of language was the removal of countless utterances from human communication as so much rubbish. Linguistic rubbish clutters the life of people in the same way in which the furniture of stuffy Victorian interiors did, or the ornaments of the pseudo-historical architecture against which modern architects like Loos or Gropius battled. By cleansing language of its pseudo-propositions, Wittgenstein hoped to gain a clarity of perception, purpose, and action which seemed to be impossible in the intellectual muddle in which Western civilization was caught.

5. A proposition is a truth-function of elementary propositions.

According to thesis number two, facts are composed of atomic facts, or "states of affairs." Similarly, ordinary propositions (which depict facts) are composed of more elementary propositions. "The book is on the table and the coffee pot on the stove," e.g., is made up of the two more elementary propositions "The book is on the table" and "The coffee pot is on the stove."

To say that propositions are "truth-functions" of elementary propositions is to say that the truth or falsity of propositions depends on (is a function of) the truth or falsity of the elementary propositions of which it is composed. If the two elementary propositions in the above example are both true, for example, then the complex proposition "The book is on the table and the coffee pot on the stove" is also true. If, however, either one of the more elementary propositions, or both of them, are false, then the complex proposition is also false.

Wittgenstein used the so-called "truth-tables" (standard equipment in today's symbolic logic) to show the dependency of the truth-value of complex propositions on their constituent elementary propositions in a systematic fashion. The part of symbolic logic which deals with the truth-functional relations between propositions is known as the "Propositional Calculus." It is Wittgenstein's contention in the *Tractatus* that the entirety of meaningful language (i.e., language dealing with facts) is governed by the laws of the Calculus. Or, to put it another way, the entirety of language can in principle be reduced to four types of propositions[10] and their interrelations according to the Calculus of Propositions. This is, of course, far from obvious if one looks at the actual multitude of kinds of propositions in ordinary languages. It seems, in fact, preposterous to maintain that ultimately they are nothing more than variations of the four basic types constructed by logicians. But it was one of the basic convictions of all early Analytic philosophers that the underlying logical structure of language was deeply hidden beneath the external variety of linguistic forms. (Wittgenstein once remarked that ordinary language reveals its true logical form as little as clothes reveal the actual shape of the body, as both are designed for quite different purposes.) The Analytic Philosopher's task was understood to be the systematic dissection of ordinary language to lay bare the hidden laws which govern its operations. And the truth-functional relation between propositions was used by Wittgenstein to this end.

An implication of this use of the Propositional Calculus in the analysis of language is the essential separateness of all facts, as is discussed in connection with the first statement of the *Tractatus*. Since connections exist only on the level of language, the assumption of connections between facts is illusory. To assume that one fact can be caused by another, e.g., is a misconception of common sense: "The belief in the causal nexus is a superstition."[11] The world is not a whole, held together by a network of connections, but a conglomerate of isolated states of affairs. It is this atomistic worldview which is ultimately supported by the Propositional Calculus, and it is one of the main reasons why its constructs figure so prominently among the central statements of the *Tractatus*.

7. *Whereof one cannot speak, thereof one must be silent.*

This last statement of the *Tractatus* is the general conclusion of all the preceding analyses and reflections. It states explicitly the purpose of the whole book. What one can speak about are facts. The attempt to speak about anything else results in senseless or nonsensical propositions.

Things about which it is impossible to speak, according to the *Tractatus*, are the "foundations" of logic, ultimate values, and metaphysics. And with the elimination of these subject matters, philosophy as traditionally understood is abolished. All that is left to do for philosophers is to show the impossibility of philosophy, i.e., to show the lack of any basis for their own existence as philosophers.

Philosophers like Russell have tried to give a rational foundation and justification for the operations of logic and mathematics. In instance after instance Wittgenstein tried to demonstrate that such a foundation and justification is both impossible and unnecessary. All one can do is show how logic (and thus mathematics) functions. Any attempt at providing a "basis" for logic will end in arbitrary assumptions, or infinite regressions.

Philosophers like Plato or Kant have tried to provide rational foundations for moral, aesthetic, and other values. The history of philosophy is full of attempts to eliminate "arbitrariness" from ethics and art criticism by deducing principles of judgment from pure reason. It is obvious that so far philosophers have met with failure. Wittgenstein's response to this situation is not to say that so far the attempts have not been good enough, nor that the principles offered by philosophers are wrong, but rather that the whole enterprise of deducing values is wrong-headed. It is impossible to live, as it were, neutrally in a world of facts and then deduce, from facts or pure reason, absolutely binding values. Rather, one evaluates things as soon as one perceives them; "evaluation" is as primary as the facts themselves. ("Ethics is transcendental," as Wittgenstein says, using Kantian terminology.) And if one finds oneself with a neutral attitude toward the affairs of the world, then this is itself already an ethical evaluation. In all this, however, philosophy has no place. Philosophy can here and there clarify a concept or a piece of reasoning, but it cannot bring about a way of life which must have its origin in things other than reason.

Metaphysicians have always tried to interpret the world in the light of something which in one way or another is "beyond" the world, "beyond" the realm of facts. They have tried to shed light on the *physics* from the vantage point of a *meta-physics*. The realm of the metaphysical has sometimes been depicted as a quasi-world beyond the world (as a *"Hinter-Welt,"* as Nietzsche put it polemically), and sometimes as a level of Being which is distinguished from the things that simply are. In the case of Plato it has been defined as the realm of *ideas* after which the things of the world of experience are patterned. What is common to all metaphysical thinking is the assumption that there is more than the world of facts, that the world is limited by something which is not part of the world. Since the realm of the metaphysical is by definition beyond experience, the history of philosophy is full of dubious assumptions and conceptual fudgings which are meant to establish its existence. Wittgenstein cut through these confused efforts by requiring that propositions be "logical pictures" of possible states of affairs, pictures which can be shown to be true or false. By relegating metaphysical statements to the kinds of propositions which are neither true nor false, i.e., without sense, he removed metaphysics from the things that can be talked about at all: "What can be said at all can be said clearly, and what we cannot talk about we must pass over in silence."[12]

With this radical departure from the aims and assumptions of traditional philosophy Wittgenstein established a new paradigm of thought, and thus inaugurated a kind of self-understanding which had its concurring expressions in the arts of the early twentieth century.

NOTES ON THE INTRODUCTION

1. Wittgenstein made two trend-setting contributions to twentieth century philosophy, first with his early work (summarized in his *Tractatus* [1921],[Ludwig Wittgenstein, *Tractatus Logico-Philosophicus,* new English translation by D.F. Pears and B.F. McGuinness,(London: Routledge & Kegan Paul, 1961), (hereafter cited as *Tractatus*)]), then with his later work (summarized in his *Philosophical Investigations* [Ludwig Wittgenstein, *Philosophical Investigations,* trans. G.E.M. Anscombe (New York: Macmillan, 1953), (hereafter cited as *Philosophical Investigations*)]). Wittgenstein's later work is in part a continuation, and in part a profound critique of his earlier work. As far as actual analytical accomplishments are concerned, his later work is of far greater importance than that of the *Tractatus* period. For the purpose of grasping the essential features of twentieth century culture, however, the simple, extreme, and dramatic conclusions of the *Tractatus* are more useful than the elaborate and complex analyses of the *Philosophical Investigations.* They are considered here not with respect to their truth or falsity, but rather as documents of twentieth century thinking.

2. Cf. Paul Engelmann, *Ludwig Wittgenstein. Briefe und Begegnungen,* (Vienna and Munich: R. Oldenbourg, 1970), the chapter on Wittgenstein and Art.

3. Wittgenstein, *Philosophical Investigations,* sections 66-77.

4. Wittgenstein, *Tractatus,* 6.432.

5. Wittgenstein, "Lecture on Ethics," 6.

6. Wittgenstein, *Tractatus,* 1.21.

7. Wittgenstein, *Philosophical Investigations,* section 60.

8. Cf. John Moran, *Toward the World and Wisdom of Wittgenstein's 'Tractatus'* (The Hague: Mouton, 1973), 75-89.

9. There are certain parallels to this in modern painting. Theo Van Doesburg in his *Principles of Neo-Plastic Art* (trans. Janet Seligman, [Greenwich, Connecticut: New York Graphic Society, 1966]), e.g., shows the transformation of a realistic object into an artistic composition. The first step is the photograph of a cow, a most simple kind of picture. The next step is a reduction of the outstanding features of the cow to a highly schematic representation of the animal. The third step is a partial re-composition of the pictorial elements of the previous version in a way which is only faintly reminiscent of the natural object. The fourth step is almost an abstract composition, only indirectly related to the photograph

of the cow. Yet, in Wittgenstein's sense of "picture" all four versions can serve as representations of the factual cow.

10. The four basic connectives are usually taken to be "and," "or," "if . . . then," and "not." In Thesis 6, Wittgenstein refers to the "Sheffer Stroke" which, as Sheffer had shown, can replace the other four connectives.

11. Wittgenstein, *Tractatus,* 5.1361.

12. *Ibid.,* Preface.

CHAPTER ONE

THE END OF
METAPHYSICS

THE END OF METAPHYSICS

Wittgenstein, in his "Lecture on Ethics" of 1929-30, makes the following remarks about metaphysical statements. ("Metaphysical" is taken here in a broad sense. It includes the language of traditional religion and theology as well as the writings of philosophical metaphysics. For the Wittgenstein of the *Tractatus* period it even includes the statements of ethics, aesthetics, and other areas of ultimate and absolute values.)

Now, I want to impress on you that a certain characteristic misuse of our language runs through *all* ethical and religious expressions. All these expressions *seem, prima facie,* to be just *similes* ... For when we speak of God and that He sees everything and when we kneel and pray to Him all our terms and actions seem to be parts of a great and elaborate allegory which represents Him as a human being of great power whose grace we try to win, etc., etc. .. Thus in ethical and religious language we seem constantly to be using similes. But a simile must be the simile for *something.* And if I can describe a fact by means of a simile I must also be able to drop the simile and to describe the facts without it. Now in our case as soon as we try to drop the simile and simply to state the facts which stand behind it, we find that there are no such facts. And so, what at first appeared to be a simile now seems to be mere nonsense.[1]

What is at issue here is the possibility or impossibility of understanding those statements in religious and other metaphysical texts which seem to be descriptions of a transcendent world, a world entirely beyond empirical experience. Wittgenstein maintains in his lecture, as in the *Tractatus*, that nobody can either believe or refuse to believe a religious statement, because it is in principle impossible to understand what it says. A religious statement looks like a statement, as it is composed of words and formed in accordance with grammatical patterns. But upon closer inspection it turns out that it has no sense, that it is a pseudo-statement — a meaningless assemblage of sounds or marks of the sort one finds in the linguistic plays of Lewis Carroll: " 'Twas brillig, and the slithy toves / Did gyre and gimble in the wabe;" (*Through The Looking Glass*). Wittgenstein's reasons for condemning metaphysical statements as pseudo-statements can be laid out as follows.

The expressions of religious language are said to be just similes, i.e, indirect descriptions of things, because there are obvious difficulties with understanding them in a direct, literal way. For example, if God "sees" everything, He obviously cannot do what human beings do when they see, for seeing in this sense involves a body, eyeballs, a suitable position for viewing, and so forth. None of these can very well be attributed to the seeing of God. There are similar difficulties with understanding God's actions, His emotional disposition, or His mind. For any of these states and activities are intelligible only in connection with physical beings and their behavior, and there are several good reasons why one should hesitate to conceive of God as such a being. The whole notion of God as a human-like being with superhuman powers to whom one submits, whose grace one tries to win, etc., is hopelessly anthropomorphic and inadequate when scrutinized closely, and thus it seems necessary to abandon the idea that religious texts describe transcendent matters in a direct way. The only way out of the above difficulties seems to be to interpret the statements of religious language as similes, as indirect descriptions of something which cannot be conveyed directly.[2] Unfortunately for religious language, however, there are considerable difficulties with this seeming way out as well.

If the expressions of religious language were similes, they would have to stand in the same relation to the transcendent matters they supposedly describe as, e.g., certain anthropomorphic expressions used for the description of machines to the machine they describe. It is possible to describe the security device of a building as if it were a superhuman person. One could say such things as "It is behaving very well tonight," or, on account of its electronic eyes, "It sees everybody entering and leaving the building." One can also say that it "admits" or "refuses entrance" to visitors, depending on whether the latter insert proper ID cards into the appropriate slots. The regulating computer of the mechanism can be said to be "startled" when fed with unforeseen data. It is clear that in this and similar cases expressions like "seeing," "behaving," "being startled," etc. are not used in a literal sense, but rather metaphorically. A building's security mechanism does not really see, etc., but rather functions in a way which in certain respects is analogous to what human beings do when they see, refuse entrance, or are startled. Thus, such expressions as "seeing" can be considered similes when they are used outside the sphere of those human activities in connection with which they are developed and normally applied.

What is important here for Wittgenstein's contention is the fact that those metaphorical expressions can be replaced by literal descriptions of what is actually happening in the above mechanism. Instead of saying that it "sees" people entering and leaving one can describe the functioning of photosensitive cells, of impulses transmitted through wires to the regulating computer, and so forth. One, in short, can describe the functioning of the installation by using either anthropomorphic or technical terms, and whenever there are questions about the former, one can have recourse to the latter. It is the possibility of such recourse to nonmetaphorical language which Wittgenstein finds lacking in the case of religious language. Thus, while it is clear that God does not see in the way human beings do, it is not clear what God does do when he "sees." In the *Tractatus* Wittgenstein writes: "To understand a proposition is to know what is the case if it is true."[3] But we do not know what is said to be the case when it is said that "God sees." It follows that we do not understand a text which says that "God sees everything." It also follows that we cannot understand whatever else is said about God's activities, dispositions, and plans as all these anthropomorphic reports fail to be translatable into direct descriptions of metaphysical events. Once scrutinized in the above analytical manner, all religious texts turn out to be without meaning. A text such as the following, to give one example, is utterly unintelligible:

And I saw a great white throne and the One seated on it. From behind Him the earth and heaven fled away, and no place was found for them. And I saw the dead, the great and the small, standing before the throne, and scrolls were opened. But another scroll was opened; it is the scroll of life, and the dead were judged out of those things written in the scrolls according to their deeds. And the sea gave up those dead in it, and death and Hades give up those dead in them, and they were judged individually according to their deeds. And death and Hades were hurled into the lake of fire. This means the second death, the lake of fire. Furthermore, whoever was not found written in the book of life was hurled into the lake of fire.[4]

Some scenes of this vision do not pose any difficulties if one sees them as real events or as poetic fantasies. An authority sitting on a throne, officials scrutinizing registers, or even a lake on fire are events which one can at least imagine. Difficulties arise when one tries to see these events as what they are meant to be, as parts of such other-worldly occurrences as a divine Last Judgment. Is it possible to even imagine a register, stored away somewhere, which lists the names and deeds of everyone who has ever lived? Can one imagine a legal machinery which could process these millions? What is one to make of Hades' being thrown into the burning lake? How can the sea give up everyone who ever perished and dissolved in it? How can an individual "live" eternally—in what form, in which location? In short: What exactly do such statements *mean?* What is one to grasp in hearing or reading them?

It is the inevitable failure to translate the statements of religious text into direct, understandable descriptions of transcendent events which leads Wittgenstein to the conclusion that the expressions of religions and other kinds of metaphysical language are "mere nonsense." Such statements are attempts to say something which cannot be said (or even thought). Language is simply not capable of performing such a feat. The attempt to put a metaphysical meaning into language is like trying to put more into a container than it can hold: ". . . our words will express only facts; as a teacup will hold only a teacup full of water, and if I were to pour a gallon over it."[5]

The exposure of metaphysical language as nonsense is one of the most dramatic and important points of the *Tractatus*. Wittgenstein, by his analysis and critique of language, intended a sweeping clean-up of philosophy and other areas of discourse. In the preface of the *Tractatus* he states: "The whole sense of the book might be summed up in the following words: What can be said at all can be said clearly, and what we cannot talk about we must pass over in silence." And the book ends with the famous conclusion: "Whereof one cannot speak, thereof one must be silent."

The purification of language from obfuscating verbiage and meaningless language is not only the stated goal of the *Tractatus,* but, according to Wittgenstein, of philosophy in general. In sections 4.114 and 4.115 one finds:

It [philosophy] must set limits to what can be thought; and, in doing so, to what cannot be thought.

It must set limits to what cannot be thought by working outward through what can be thought. It will signify what cannot be said by presenting clearly what can be said.

On the basis of this conception of philosophy and language no representation of a transcendent, supernatural world is possible. A positive, revealed religion with its cosmogeny, prophesies, and dogmas was literally unthinkable and unsayable for Wittgenstein. He could, e.g., not grasp the conception of God as creator of the world, let alone believe in such a God. And although he himself was raised as a Catholic, with reference to two of his friends who had converted to Catholicism Wittgenstein said: "I could not possibly bring myself to believe all the things that they believe."[6] The idea of a transcendent world, which had dominated so much of Western thought up to the twentieth century, was not just an empirical improbability, but a logical impossibility for the author of the *Tractatus*. In his view of the world Wittgenstein was a strict immanentist.

Yet, while insisting that all metaphysical statements are without sense, Wittgenstein also writes in the *Tractatus:* "There is indeed the inexpressible. It *shows* itself; it is the mystical."[7] And in a letter to Ludwig von Ficker, Wittgenstein comments on the *Tractatus* as follows:

> Once I planned to add something to the preface which now is not in it. I wanted to write that my work consists of two parts: of the part which is actually there, and the other part which I have *not* written. And it is the second part which is the important one . . . All that about which people produce gibberish I have fixed in my book by being silent about it.[8]

Hence, that about which one cannot talk, "the mystical," does not only exist, "showing itself," but also carries very much weight with the author of the *Tractatus*. Wittgenstein, in other words, does not seem to entirely rule out a transcendence; his view of the world does not seem to be entirely immanentist, after all.

Mentioning of the "mystical" seems problematic in the light of the *Tractatus'* position concerning metaphysics. It seems to surreptitiously re-introduce the very things which Wittgenstein's critique of language ruled out as nonsensical. It seems, in fact, so alien to the spirit of the *Tractatus* that the members of the Vienna Circle (as well as other Logical Positivists) simply ignored it, although in all other respects they considered Wittgenstein's book as one of their major sources of inspiration.

It should be observed, however, that Wittgenstein did not introduce the "mystical" as something like a transcendent realm, as a quasi-world beyond the world. "What is mystical" is not a peculiar range of objects. To understand what Wittgenstein means by it one has to stay clear of the temptation to think of the mystical on the model of "things". (For this reason the translation of section 6.522 by D.F. Pears and B.F. McGuinness may for some readers be misleading. This translation reads: "There are, indeed, things that cannot be put into words. They make themselves manifest. They are what is mystical." This way of putting it may be somewhat too suggestive of quasi-facts beyond the world.)

The "mystical," according to the *Tractatus,* is not a realm of transcendent things, but a special way of relating to the world; it is a "feeling":

> To view the world *sub specie aeterni* is to view it as a whole—a limited whole.
> Feeling the world as a limited whole—it is this that is the mystical.[9]

The question is what it means to view or feel the world as "a limited whole".

The notion of perceiving the world as a "whole" is elucidated in those remarks of the *Notebooks* in which Wittgenstein explains "the view *sub specie aeternitatis*" (the "viewpoint of eternity"): "The usual way of looking at things sees objects as it were from the midst of them, the view *sub specie aeternitatis* from outside."[10] To see things from the midst of them is to have the kind of closeness to things which comes with pragmatic, every day involvement. When concerned with the construction of a dwelling, e.g., a builder will see trees primarily as lumber, or when concerned with real estate development, a landscape will be seen by him as a suitable or unsuitable site for a plant, etc. This perception of the world is limited by special needs, and its duration ceases with its practical purpose. In this sense it is narrow-minded and short-sighted. It is the opposite of the "viewpoint of eternity".

This pragmatic perception has traditionally been contrasted with another, entirely different approach, namely aesthetic perception. The aesthete's way of seeing the world is primarily characterized by its lack of practical involvement, by its disinterestedness. The aesthete's basic attitude is not active and practical, but passive and contemplative. The aesthete puts, so to speak, a considerable distance between himself (his personal needs and interests) and the things which he perceives. Instead of seeing only selected and limited aspects of the world, the aesthete has a god-like view: he sees the world as a whole.

In the *Tractatus* Wittgenstein advocates a view of the world which is characterized by this aesthetic distance. The contemplative disinterestedness which is typical for the perception of works of art is generalized by Wittgenstein into an attitude toward the whole world:

> The work of art is the object seen *sub specie aeternitatis;* and the good life is the world seen *sub specie aeternitatis.*[11]

This is the connection between art and ethics. To see the world as a whole is to see it from a great distance, from the viewpoint of one who has extricated himself or herself from the practical affairs of the world.

(The theme of the viewer's distance from the world is discussed by Wittgenstein not only in connection with art and aesthetics, but even more so with morality. In his "Lecture on Ethics" Wittgenstein states: "The murder will be on exactly the same level as any other event, for instance the falling of a stone."[12] The full meaning of this statement will be discussed in Chapter II. For the time being it should be noticed, however, how extraordinarily distant [how little "in the midst of things"] someone must be to see a murder and a falling stone as equally significant or insignificant events.)

As the notion of seeing the world as a whole, the idea of seeing the world as a *"limited"* whole is also connected with the unworldliness at which Wittgenstein aims, although in a somewhat different way. At the beginning of the *Tractatus* Wittgenstein writes: "The world is all that is the case.—The world is the totality of facts, . . ." This statement is, among other things, a delineation of what there is, of what one can talk about without producing nonsense. It is a statement of the ontology which accompanies Wittgenstein's theory of language. Yet, Wittgenstein is aware of a "tendency in the human mind" which prompts people to try to transcend the world of facts, to try to say things which cannot be said. His "Lecture on Ethics" ends with the words:

> For all I wanted to do with them [the expressions of metaphysical language] was just *to go beyond* the world, and that is to say beyond significant language. My whole tendency, and I believe the tendency of all men who ever tried to write or talk Ethics or Religion, was to run against the boundaries of language. This running against the wall of our cage is perfectly, absolutely hopeless. Ethics, so far as it springs from the desire to say something about the ultimate meaning of life, the absolute good, the absolute valuable, can be no science. What it says does not add to our knowledge in any sense. But it is a document of a tendency in the human mind which I personally cannot help

respecting deeply, and I would not for my life ridicule it.[13]

This "tendency" prompts metaphysically inclined thinkers to deny what is stated at the beginning of the *Tractatus,* namely that the world is all that is the case. A hallmark of a religious attitude is the conviction that there must be something besides mere facts, that the world of experience cannot be all there is, that there must be a transcendent existence beyond the world. In the *Notebooks* Wittgenstein writes: "To believe in God means to see that the facts of the world are not the end of the matter."[14] From a religious point of view, the world is limited by something which is not part of the world: the transcendence constitutes the limit of the world of facts.

This is, to be sure, sheer nonsense as far as the *Tractatus* is concerned. For this reason the "view of the world *sub specie aeterni*" is a "feeling" rather than a theoretical position. But what prompts the production of this nonsense is given considerable weight and respect in those passages of Wittgenstein's writings which deal with the "mystical" and related issues. The *Notebooks* in particular give ample testimony of how seriously and intensively Wittgenstein struggled to come to terms with a religious view of the world. In a certain sense Wittgenstein can be said to have lived a religious life—in spite of his rejection of metaphysics. Henrik von Wright writes in his "Biographical Sketch" of Wittgenstein: "Certainly he did not have a Christian faith."[15] And Norman Malcolm writes in his *Memoir:* "I do not wish to give the impression that Wittgenstein accepted any religious faith—he certainly did not—or that he was a religious person."[16] But von Wright adds to his remark: "But neither was his view of life unchristian, pagan, as was Goethe's."[17] And Malcolm adds to his: "But I think that there was in him, in some sense, the *possibility* of religion."[18]

Paul Engelmann records both Wittgenstein's violent rejection of all "transcendent hogwash," and his strong attraction to a religious point of view. Thus, on the one hand Wittgenstein writes in a letter to Engelmann:

> When you say that I have no faith you are quite right, but I have never had it. It is, after all, quite clear that a person who wants, so to speak, to invent a machine which makes him decent, has no faith. But what can I do? One thing is clear to me: I am far too evil to produce subtle theories about myself. I either remain a swinish creature, or I become a better person—and that's all there is to it! No transcendent hogwash, if everything is as clear as a slap in the face![19]

On the other hand Engelmann recounts: "Wittgenstein has, at least during the time in which I knew him, revered Tolstoy to the utmost, and among Tolstoy's writings, besides *The Gospel in Brief,* his *Popular Stories.*"[20] And in a letter to Ludwig von Ficker, Wittgenstein credits Tolstoy's *Gospel* with having almost saved his life,[21] while his sister Hermine records that among soldiers during World War I, Wittgenstein was known as "the one with the Bible".[22]

The "possibility of religion" is reflected in a great many other details of Wittgenstein's life style and conduct as well. In several of his published letters from the *Tractatus* period, one finds such concluding phrases as "God be with you," and in a letter to von Ficker he writes: "If I had only already found another place for myself than this shitty world!"[23] In the mid-twenties Wittgenstein worked for awhile as a gardener in a monastery near Vienna, and he actually considered becoming a monk. It was presumably only the lack of a positive faith which prevented the realization of this plan.[24] After World War I Wittgenstein converted to a lifestyle of extreme simplicity, a lifestyle which in several ways resembled that of monks. And Malcolm's description of Wittgenstein's room at Cambridge University bears a striking resemblance to that of a monk's cell.

What in the end has to be recognized as characteristic of the *Tractatus* and the mind of its author is neither the plain positivistic rejection of metaphysics, nor the unproblematic acceptance of religion, but rather the extraordinary tension between the passionate desire to transcend the world of facts, and a relentless intellectual honesty which made any metaphysics impossible. Wittgenstein was more ardently religious than the average member of any church, and at the same time more critical and rationalistic than the traditional advocate of Enlightenment and Reason. He was religious without having any faith, and he renounced the world, in the way of monks, without having the consolation of a world beyond the world of facts. He related to the world as if it were limited by a transcendence, but he bore in mind that this transcendence was void.

It may seem problematic to both hold the view that the world of facts is all there is, and at the same time relate to the world as if it were limited by a transcendence, as if there were a world beyond the world in favor of which one could neglect the latter. If one believes that this world is all that is the case, a critic may argue, then one cannot be a religious person. And if one really lives like a religious person, then one has to assume that there is more than this world. To combine an immanentist view of the world with a religious attitude seems to amount to a contradiction, i.e., to a logical impossibility.

But this criticism is based on a questionable assumption concerning the relation between what one believes and how one acts. According to this assumption, there must be a strict coherence between one's beliefs and one's behaviour, a coherence which is usually expressed by saying that actions reflect one's belief, or that actions grow out of one's understanding of the world. Wittgenstein rejects this assumption. For him, people's actions, attitudes, dispositions, or feelings are not necessarily consequences of certain beliefs, but either come about independently of any beliefs, or even generate the latter. Beliefs may reflect certain practical attitudes and forms of behaviour, but they may also simply accompany one's conduct without having much to do with it, or they may even be lacking altogether. How one lives or feels is in principle independent of what one thinks and of what one says. Thus in a discussion with members of the Vienna Circle, Wittgenstein states:

> Is talking essential for religion? I can easily imagine a religion in which there are no doctrines, in which, therefore, no talking occurs. Obviously, the essence of religion cannot have anything to do with the fact that talking occurs, or rather: if talking occurs, then this is itself part of the religious act, and not a theory. And it does not matter, therefore, whether such words are true, false, or nonsensical.[26]

It is because people have certain attitudes and feelings that they say and "believe" certain things, not the other way around. People do not read John's vision and then become afraid of a Last Judgment, rather they feel guilty and therefore may have visions of or are interested in reading about such a Judgment. And since this interest is maintained by their inner dispositions, the visions are not scrutinized with respect to historical evidence or logical intelligibility. The visions are an expression of an original disposition, and they may or may not be part of an established conduct.

This primacy of practice is also expressed in the words of Jesus according to Tolstoy's *Gospel:* "You do not believe because you do not follow me."[27] What Tolstoy's Jesus emphasizes is that the following, the religious commitment, comes first, and only then the content of faith. And it is clear that the content of any faith, the special dogmas and prophesies, are secondary in importance to one's basic attitude toward life. Tolstoy expresses this in *A Confession* as follows:

No argument could convince me of the truth of their faith. Only deeds which showed that they saw a meaning in life making what was so dreadful to me—poverty, sickness, and death—not dreadful to them, could convince me.[28]

It stands to reason that it was Tolstoy's emphasis on practice and a way of life which made such a great impression on Wittgenstein at the time when he read *The Gospel in Brief.* It coincides entirely with his own understanding of the relation between practice and belief, and it illustrates how a religious life can be lived regardless of the intelligibility or unintelligibility of metaphysical texts. The transcendence may be void, but that does not mean that one has to feel at home in this world.

Kafka: "On Similes"

Franz Kafka was born in Prague in 1883. He studied law and made a living as an employee of insurance companies in his home town. He wrote in his spare time; only short stories were published during his lifetime. In 1917 it was discovered that he had tuberculosis. He succumbed to the disease in 1924. During the last years of his life he lived in Berlin, where he wrote as much as his condition allowed.

In Prague, as in most areas of the multi-national Hapsburg empire, ethnic Germans were a politically and culturally dominant minority. Kafka, of Jewish origin, was part of a minority within a minority. He was educated in the classical German tradition, and he wrote German in a predominantly Czech environment. The significance of his work, however, is only very indirectly related to the ethnic and political turmoil of the last years of the Hapsburg monarchy. His major theme is the human condition of the modern age. His stories are classics of modern literature—both on account of their exploration of modern alienation, and on account of their nonrealistic prose.

Kafka's most often anthologized short stories, both published during his lifetime, are "The Metamorphosis" (1915), and "In the Penal Colony" (1919). His novels, all fragments, are *Amerika, The Trial,* and *The Castle.* In his will, Kafka stipulated that all unpublished materials be burned after his death. His friend and literary executor Max Brod did not comply with this wish, and thus saved some of the most outstanding writings of modern literature.

"On Similes" ("Von den Gleichnissen")[29] is one of Kafka's shortest and most intriguing pieces. It was written around 1922-23, and never published during the author's lifetime. It deals with the relation between metaphysical statements and practical conduct. Its point parallels the one made by Wittgenstein.

ON SIMILES

Many complain that the words of the wise are always only similes, but unusable in everyday life—and that is the only life we have. When the wise man says: "Go beyond," then he does not mean that one should go to the other side, which one could certainly do if the result of going would be worth it—but he means some legendary beyond, something we do not know, which he himself could not determine any more specifically, and which therefore is of no help to us here. All these similes really want to say only that what cannot be grasped cannot be grasped, and that we knew already. But what we labor on every day are other things.

To this someone said: "Why do you resist? If you would follow the similes you would have become similes yourself, and thus already be free of your daily drudgery."

Someone else said: "I bet this is a simile too."

The first said: "You win."

The second said: "But unfortunately only in the simile."

The first said: "No, in reality; in the simile you lose."

Those who complain about the words of the wise complain about their unintelligibility. When the wise man says: "Go beyond," then clearly he does not mean this in any literal sense —as if he had said: "Go to the other side of this river," or: "Go to another part of the world," or even: "Go beyond your individual, material interests." To "go beyond" in the sense suggested by the wise seems to refer to a realm which lies beyond everything that can be described in language—and thus it does not seem to mean anything at all. The difficulties concerning the determination of the "legendary beyond" are obviously the same as those arising in connection with the description of anything transcendent: the expressions used in pointing to the transcendent seem to be used like expressions used to point to some area of the world, yet it is clear that the transcendent cannot be anything like an area of the world. (If the transcendent were not radically different from the world one would not know where to draw the line between the world and what lies beyond.) Consequently, the words of the wise do not seem to convey anything, they seem to be "useless."

The whole line of thought implied in Wittgenstein's philosophy and alluded to in the first part of Kafka's "On Similes" is challenged by the remark of the first speaker in Kafka's piece. The first speaker's reply to the foregoing complaints is: "Why do you resist? If you would follow the similes you would become similes yourself, and thus already be free of your daily drudgery." What this speaker is suggesting, in other words, is to ignore the above difficulties and to *follow* the words of the wise and the visions these words conjure up. That is, the point of the words of the wise is not to describe a transcendent world, but rather to encourage acting or living in a certain way. One can, after all, very well live *as if* one will be held accountable for one's actions, no matter whether a transcendent world with quasi-authorities and quasi-judgments is intelligible or not. The point of the words of the wise is *practical* in this sense, not *theoretical.* (It is the sceptic's attention that is caught by the mysteries of the "legendary beyond;" the follower of the words of the wise is concerned with acting here and now.) By living and acting in a certain way the follower of the words of the wise will encourage others to do likewise, that is he will "become a simile himself" by being an example to be emulated by others.

The second speaker, not seeing the (practical) point of the words of the wise, i.e., still thinking that the words of the wise are an attempted metaphorical description of a transcendent world, responds by saying that the first speaker's advice, namely to *follow* the words of the wise, must be a simile itself—which is confirmed by the first speaker. What the second speaker has in mind is the idea that the first speaker's advice is of the same sort as the words of the wise, more specifically, that it is as problematic as what the wise men say. For if it is true that the words of the wise are unintelligible, then it seems clear that to speak of following these words is unintelligible, too. (If the notion of a future Judgment is unintelligible, than it seems irrational to prepare oneself for such an event.) To underline his sceptical opinion about the words of the wise the second speaker continues the dialogue by modifying his first characterization of the first speaker's remark. He maintains that he was right in calling that remark a simile "only in the simile," i.e., only from the standpoint of someone who thinks the words of the wise really have a metaphorical meaning. (He assumes that that is what the first speaker and the followers of the words of the wise believe.) For sceptics like the second speaker himself, however, as well as for all who complain about the words of the wise, his first characterization must be invalid, since the idea of a metaphorical meaning of the words of the wise turned out to be an illusion.

At this point the first speaker states that the second speaker was mistaken all along, and mistaken in a much more fundamental way than the second speaker himself ever suspected he could be. Throughout the dialogue the second speaker took it for granted that the difference at issue was the difference between believing that the words of the wise are metaphorical descriptions of transcendent matters on the one hand, and believing that they are "mere nonsense" on the other. The first speaker's final remark reveals that the real difference at issue is between construing the words of the wise as descriptions of transcendent matters at all, whether as successful descriptions or failing ones, and taking them as expressions of a different nature all together. According to the first speaker, as has been indicated earlier, the words of the wise are neither successful nor failing descriptions of a transcendent world, but statements whose significance is entirely practical. To elucidate how these words can be practical without being intelligible descriptions of transcendent matters, it will be helpful to compare them with the statues and images of God found in places of worship. It would obviously be wrong-headed to look at such statues and images as attempts to picture God,[30] as attempted portraits, as it were, whose likeness could be tested at a future date by an act of eschatological verification. The function of such statutes and images is rather to remind, exhort, or awe people who participate in a certain way of life. Similarly, such things as John's vision of the Last Judgment are not scenarios or a panorama of future transcendent happenings, but expressions of how people engaged in a certain way of life conceive of themselves, reminders of the limits of life on earth, etc. The first speaker's final remark, in short, is a criticism of the position of the second speaker and of all those who complain about the unintelligibility of the words of the wise. The first speaker points out by his final remark that all those who find the words of the wise unintelligible expect something from these words which by their nature they cannot give, and which they are not meant to give. Those who look at the words of the wise as possible descriptions of a transcendent world commit, according to the first speaker, a category mistake, and the course of the dialogue in Kafka's piece shows that nothing further said by the wise will succeed in making the original words more understandable, unless the above misconception is overcome, and people see what *kind* of words the words of the wise are. Recognition of the category mistake involved in the dialogue of the piece could be called the point of Kafka's "On Similes."

Kafka's story reflects on a situation in which metaphysically inclined people try to come to terms with statements which seem to refer to a transcendent world, a world which cannot be grasped. The story suggests that it is a mistake to dismiss such statements as unintelligible, because this dismissal is based on a misunderstanding. The proper way to understand "the words of the wise" is to see that they concern practical matters here and now, not any attempted descriptions of a transcendent world. The story suggests, in other words, that one can "go beyond," that one can act as if one transcended the world of facts, that one need not be immobilized by the impossibility to grasp the transcendence. The transcendence, the "beyond" as traditionally understood, is void, but that does not imply that one cannot "go beyond."

Trakl: "De Profundis"

Georg Trakl was born in Salzburg, Austria in 1887. He was a pharmacist by profession, but his main interest was poetry. In 1912 he found a patron and publisher in Ludwig von Ficker, editor of the periodical *Der Brenner*. Through the mediation of von Ficker, Trakl became one of the principal beneficiaries of the anonymous donation which Ludwig Wittgenstein made on behalf of needy Austrian writers. At the beginning of World War I, Trakl was drafted and stationed with the medical corps in Galicia. The experience of not being able to help the large number of casualties in his care provoked a nervous breakdown. While confined to an observation cell in a military hospital in Krakow, he died of an overdose of cocain in November 1914.

Trakl was the most outstanding poet of German literary Expressionism. His work was strongly influenced by modern French poetry, particularly by Rimbaud. Trakl's extremely melancholic condition made him a regular user of drugs and alcohol. Although his literary techniques (which he consciously studied and cultivated) cannot be entirely explained by his use of hallucinogenic drugs, there is a significant relationship between his use of such drugs and the visionary quality of his poetry.

(Wittgenstein never met Trakl, although von Ficker kept him informed about the poet. In a note to von Ficker, Wittgenstein writes: "Thank you for sending me the poems by Trakl. I do not understand them; but their *tone* elates me. It is the tone of truly genial persons."[31] When Wittgenstein learned in November 1914 that Trakl was in Krakow, close to where he himself was stationed, he immediately tried to visit him. He missed him by a few days.)

Trakl's poem "De Profundis"[32] was written in 1913. It's Latin title means "Out of the depth." Poems of this title were written by many poets. They all refer to the 130th Psalm, a prayer for redemption in a situation of utter despair:

Out of the depth I have called upon you, Jehovah.
O Jehovah, do hear my voice!
May your ears be attentive to the voice of my pleas . . .

Let Israel keep waiting for Jehovah.
For there is loving kindness with Him,
And abundant redemption.
Jehovah himself will redeem
Israel out of its errors.

Trakl's poem shares with this prayer the situation of deep despair out of which its words are spoken. Trakl's world is one which stands in urgent need of redemption. What distinguishes the modern poem from the ancient prayer, however, is the fact that the help from above is not forthcoming, that the unbroken communication with God, which is implied in the Psalm, does not take place in the world of the poem: "God's silence I drank from the well in the sylvan glade." The modern poet still conceives of the idea of a saving transcendence, his world is not left to its own devices, but this transcendence does not respond. In the end the despair of the world is all there is.

DE PROFUNDIS

There is a stubble-land in which a black rain falls.
There is a withered tree that stands alone.
There is a hissing wind that circles empty cabins.
How sad this evening.

Passing the hamlet
The gentle orphan still collects the leftover ears of grain.
Her eyes graze round and golden in the dark,
Her womb awaits the bridegroom from above.

Returning home
The shepherds found her sweet
Body rotting in the thorny bush.

I am a shadow—roaming far from gloomy villages.
God's silence
I drank from the well in the sylvan glade.

Cold metal appears on my brow.
Spiders look for my heart.
There is a light which is extinguished in my mouth.

At night I found myself in a moor,
Encrusted with trash and the dust of stars.
In the hazel bushes
Angels of crystal sounded again.

"De Profundis" is a free verse poem. Its grammatical structure is extremely simple: short, descriptive sentences are added to each other. The tone of the poem is almost laconic. But the absence of elaborate rhetorical devices makes the extraordinary starkness of the described situation all the more visible.

The poem compiles images of darkness, emptiness, and desolation: a harvested field, black rain, a lone tree, empty dwellings, an orphan, the end of the day, the end of the summer, and so forth. The orphan waits for her bridegroom to end her aloneness. The bridegroom is to be heavenly, thus uniting, as it were, the forces of heaven and earth, creating a cosmic harmony. Instead the orphan is murdered. Shepherds (possibly an allusion to the shepherds who saw the star of Bethlehem) find her rotting corpse in a thorny bush (possibly a reference to the crown of thorns put on Jesus). The guiding idea here is: thwarted redemption.

The poet is represented as a shadow, i.e., as someone who is and is not part of the world. His roaming afar from the villages indicates social isolation. This isolation is in part loneliness, but it also coincides with the solitary role of the seer, shaman, or priest. Social isolation is one of the prominent means by which such persons obtain their special insights. That the poet is conceived here as something like a seer or priest is suggested by the sylvan glade and the (sacred) well, things which have a long-standing tradition as ritual locations.

But the seer-poet's quest is in vain: God does not reveal himself; the depth of the well (symbol of the access to the inner secrets of the earth) remains silent. The seer-poet, in turn, has nothing to say either: The light (an old symbol of Enlightenment) is extinguished in his mouth. What the poet experiences falls short of divine wisdom. All there is are bodily suffering (indicated by the cold sweat on his brow) and fierce anxiety ("spiders look for my heart"). The modern priest fails to show the way to redemption.

The poem ends with depreciating the experience of the poet altogether. The poet finds himself in the wilderness, in a state which strongly suggests the coming down after a bout of intoxication. The intoxication is reminiscent of the sacred trance of the shaman, to which the "dust of stars" may allude, but also of the futile escape of a skid row drunk ("encrusted with trash"). The mentioning of angels implies another reference to traditional religion, but the text says "angels of crystal," which clearly marks the image as a personal vision of the poet, not as a description of transcendent beings. (It may even be possible that the "crystals" refer to cocain as the origin of the poet's vision.) The final situation of the poet is his awakening in the unredeemed world, and the laconic statement of his theologically impotent visions. Both the poet and the world are condemned to remain in the depth of their despair.

Eliot: *The Waste Land*

Thomas Stearns Eliot was born in St. Louis, Missouri in 1888. He received his MA degree from Harvard University in 1910. In 1915 he married and settled in England, and shortly afterwards published his first poems, *Prufrock and Other Observations* (1917). The period of 1912-1922 was the time when the Imagist movement cultivated modernism in English poetry, and Eliot was significantly influenced by the main spokesman of Imagism, Ezra Pound. In 1922 appeared Eliot's *The Waste Land,* one of the classics of modern literature. In it Eliot presented all the major themes of the modern intellectual experience: the total collapse of tradition, the disintegration of a coherent worldview, the disorientation of the self, and the lack of a transcendent, unifying perspective. In 1927 Eliot opted for a conscious return to tradition and conservative authority as an antidote for the anarchic tendencies of the modern age, and he gave external expression to this decision by becoming confirmed in the Anglican Church, and by becoming a British subject. In 1928 he described himself as a "royalist in politics, a classicist in literature, and an

Anglo-Catholic in religion." In terms of status and public honors, Eliot's life became very successful. He continued to produce highly regarded work. From 1927 onward, however, he ceased to be in the vanguard of modern literature. He died in 1965.

The following text is the first part of *The Waste Land*.[33] It describes the modern world as a barren desert, a civilization of "rubbish," in which the individual is hopelessly lost. This world needs redemption, but a transcendent force which could accomplish this is not in sight. Traditional religion is as much exhausted, scattered, and decayed as everything else in modern civilization. Thus the poet finds himself in a world in which he is not at all at home, but from which there is also no way to escape.

THE BURIAL OF THE DEAD

April is the cruellest month, breeding
Lilacs out of the dead land, mixing
Memory and desire, stirring
Dull roots with spring rain.
Winter kept us warm, covering
Earth in forgetful snow, feeding
A little life with dried tubers.
Summer surprised us, coming over the Starnbergersee
With a shower of rain; we stopped in the colonnade,
And went on in sunlight, into the Hofgarten,
And drank coffee, and talked for an hour.
Bin gar keine Russin, stamm' aus Litauen, echt deutsch.
And when we were children, staying at the arch-duke's,
My cousin's, he took me out on a sled,
And I was frightened. He said, Marie,
Marie, hold on tight. And down we went.
In the mountains, there you feel free.
I read, much of the night, and go south in the winter.

What are the roots that clutch, what branches grow
Out of this stony rubbish? Son of man,
You cannot say, or guess, for you know only
A heap of broken images, where the sun beats,
And the dead tree gives no shelter, the cricket no relief,
And the dry stone no sound of water. Only

There is shadow under this red rock,
(Come in under the shadow of this red rock),
And I will show you something different from either
Your shadow at morning striding behind you
Or your shadow at evening rising to meet you;
I will show you fear in a handful of dust.

> *Frisch weht der Wind*
> *Der Heimat zu.*
> *Mein irisch Kind,*
> *Wo weilest du?*

'You gave me hyacinths first a year ago;
'They called me the hyacinth girl.'
—Yet when we came back, late, from the Hyacinth garden,
Your arms full, and your hair wet, I could not
Speak, and my eyes failed, I was neither
Living nor dead, and I knew nothing,
Looking into the heart of light, the silence.
Öd' und leer das Meer.

Madame Sosostris, famous clairvoyante,
Had a bad cold, nevertheless
Is known to be the wisest woman in Europe,
With a wicked pack of cards. Here, said she,
Is your card, the drowned Phoenician Sailor,
(Those are pearls that were his eyes. Look!)
Here is Belladonna, the Lady of the Rocks,
The lady of situations.
Here is the man with three staves, and here the Wheel,
And here is the one-eyed merchant, and this card,
Which is blank, is something he carries on his back,
Which I am forbidden to see. I do not find
The Hanged Man. Fear death by water.
I see crowds of people, walking round in a ring.
Thank you. If you see dear Mrs. Equitone,
Tell her I bring the horoscope myself:
One must be so careful these days.

Unreal City,
Under the brown fog of a winter dawn,
A crowd flowed over London Bridge, so many,
I had not thought death had undone so many.
Sighs, short and infrequent, were exhaled,
And each man fixed his eyes before his feet.
Flowed up the hill and down King William Street,
To where Saint Mary Woolnoth kept the hours
With a dead sound on the final stroke of nine.
There I saw one I knew, and stopped him, crying: 'Stetson!
'You who were with me in the ships at Mylae!
'That corpse you planted last year in your garden,
'Has it begun to sprout? Will it bloom this year?
'Or has the sudden frost disturbed its bed?
'Oh keep the Dog far hence, that's friend to men,
'Or with his nails he'll dig it up again!
'You! hypocrite lecteur!—mon semblable,—mon frere!'

The nature of the modern world as perceived by the poet is reflected in the style and structure of *The Waste Land*. The poem is not composed in accordance with any classical and traditional form, lacks a unified language, and does not reveal an authoritative and comprehensive worldview. Rather, it is a sprawling collage of a disorienting variety of styles, languages, myths, viewpoints, and historical epochs. The poem is what, according to Eliot, all of modern civilization is: "a heap of broken images." In its entirety *The Waste Land* contains phrases in Greek, Latin, Italian, German, French and English. It uses Hebrew, Greek, Roman, Celtic, Germanic, and several Oriental mythologies. It quotes or alludes to dozens of works of world literature. It covers the epochs of Antiquity, the Middle Ages, recent centuries, and the contemporary world. Geographically it moves over many parts of the globe. It deals with the most sublime problems of culture, as well as with the most trivial details of everyday life. People of all social classes appear in it. The poet speaks with his own words, through quotations, or by means of multi-faceted allusions. His topics are inner feelings, external conditions, or abstract reflections. *The Waste Land,* in other words, offers the same dazzling variety of disparate stimuli as the fragmented world of twentieth century civilization about which it talks. It is a labyrinthean microcosm which mirrors in its complex structure the landscape of modern alienation. It could be called a blueprint of a modern Tower of Babel.

A fulfilling life has become impossible in the waste land of modern civilization. The anarchic overabundance of knowledge, cultures, life styles, goals and ideologies has rendered modern individuals directionless, noncommittal, uninspired, and stagnant. They are free of the discipline and obligations of older value systems or religions, but their lives have also lost intensity and purpose. From the disintegration of the premodern world did not emerge a new vision, but an all-pervasive emptiness:

> What are the roots that clutch, what branches grow
> Out of this stony rubbish? Son of man,
> You cannot say, or guess, for you know only
> A heap of broken images, . . .

The address "Son of man" stems from Ezekiel II, 2 ff. where God addresses the prophet with these words. In the Old Testament the situation was also one where a whole society had gone astray. But Ezekiel received clear instructions from God as to how to rectify the situation. In the modern world no such instructions are available. The twentieth century prophet faced with the modern waste land cannot even "guess" what is to come of the present chaos. One of the characteristic features of the modern world is exactly that there is no authoritative voice any more that would determine what is to be done.

To turn back to any of the myths, religions, or value systems of the past is unconvincing and futile. The thorough knowledge of so many worldviews, together with their historical genesis, relativizes every one of them. To declare one of them as the sole truth, or superior to all others, would betray a naivete which seems to be justifiable only on the basis of willful ignorance. Besides, the ancient myths and religions have suffered from degeneration under the conditions of the modern world. The archetypal figure of the seer or prophet, e.g., appears in the poem as the commercially operating Madame Sosostris with her "wicked pack of cards." In their confusion and helplessness people do turn to her, but her status can hardly be compared to that of her predecessors in pre-modern communities.

The theme of basic unfulfillment is strongly alluded to by the various quotations (in German) from Richard Wagner's opera *Tristan und Isolde.* The overall point of this opera is the idea that the fulfillment of love is impossible in life, that life can only be the yearning for fulfillment, and that the consummation of love is identical with death. This point is reflected throughout *The Waste Land* and in a certain sense it can be called the point of Eliot's poem. It is also reflected, for example, in the failing love story which is indicated by the lines:

'You gave me hyacinths first a year ago; . . .
Yet when we came back . . . I could not
Speak, and your eyes failed, I was neither
Living nor dead, and I knew nothing, . . .

The failing of love represents the failing of life in the waste land. It depicts a state of being neither fully alive nor dead. It represents a way of life which corresponds to the "rubbish" of modern civilization. That this state is central to the whole of *The Waste Land* is shown by the fact that Eliot prefaces the whole poem with a quotation from Petronius' *Satyricon* which thematizes the state of being neither alive nor dead:

For I saw with my own eyes the Sibyl hanging in a jar at Cumae, and when the acolytes asked, 'Sibyl, what do you want?' she replied, 'I want to die!' [34]

The Sibyl of Cumae was a very prominent seer in Ancient Greece. Apollo granted her the wish to live eternally. The seer unfortunately neglected to stipulate that eternal youth go along with eternal life. Thus, with the passing of time, the Sibyl shriveled into an ever smaller size, until she was small enough to reside in a jar. In this way she lived on, without being really alive. It is the horror of this fate which Eliot attributes to the existence of modern man, both in its general and personal manifestations.

The theme of being neither alive nor dead reappears further in the description of the London crowd following "Unreal City. . ." The line "I had not thought that death had undone so many" refers to an almost identical line in Dante's *Comedia Divina*. In the part of hell which Dante describes in that passage there are those who have avoided in life to choose between good and evil, and who are therefore neither welcome in hell nor in heaven. They reside just inside the gate of hell. And the line "Sighs . . . were exhaled" refers to the part of hell described by Dante where the pagans reside who had never heard of the Gospel while they were alive. They are condemned to "Limbo," where they do not suffer pain, but where they also have no hope for salvation. The ambiguous situation of both groups, again, describes the state of mind of those who inhabit the modern waste land. It is the situation of people who have avoided extremes and commitments, whose state was one of chosen or imposed indifference, and who therefore failed to be alive in the fullest sense of the word.

Downtown London, one of the very centers of the modern world, is characterized as an "unreal city." Bertrand Russell, a friend of Eliot's, describes an experience in his *Autobiography* which, according to him, inspired this passage in *The Waste Land.* In reference to his watching the busy London crowds on the eve of World War I, Russell writes:

> I used to have strange visions of London as a place of unreality. I used in imagination to see the bridges collapse and sink, and the whole great city vanish like a morning mist. Its inhabitants began to seem like hallucinations, and I would wonder whether the world in which I had thought I had lived was a mere product of my own febrile nightmares.[35]

What makes such an experience relevant for what Eliot wants to say is, of course, not the occasional febrility of this or that state of mind, but the idea of the thorough insubstantiality of the way of life which Western civilization has developed. The crowds are busy like ants, and every individual in the crowd acts as if his or her business were of the utmost importance, but nobody seems to be able to explain what the whole gigantic process, that is symbolized by the London crowds, is about. Narrow-mindedness keeps everyone in line ("And each man fixed his eyes before his feet"). But when the ultimate purpose of the process of production, consumption, and destruction which has been created by the modern age is questioned, then observers like Russell or Eliot can experience the feeling of unreality in view of the twentieth century metropolis with its overwhelming masses of people and goods.

Although no transcendence appears in "The Burial of the Dead," Eliot's description of the modern world is not immanentist. He assembles a great number of facts in his text, but the facts are constantly transcended by means of allusions which seem to open up a realm beyond the here and now. Biblical allusions are particularly telling in this respect. The following lines may serve as an example:

Saint Mary Woolnoth kept the hours
With a dead sound on the final stroke of nine.

Saint Mary Woolnoth is a London church. The Christian nature of the building, and the words "dead," "final," and "nine" suggest a reference to the death of Jesus who in the ninth hour of his agony cried out: "My God, why hast thou forsaken me?" It is clear that the hour of Jesus' deepest despair corresponds to the modern waste land, which is thus characterized as a god-forsaken civilization. Jesus was finally redeemed and went to heaven. In *The Waste Land* no such redemption occurs. The Christian faith is as much part of the "heap of broken images" as any other cultural tradition. Yet, it is clear that the world is viewed by the poet as if it stood in need of redemption, as if there were a salvation which it cannot obtain. The poet perceives the world as if it were "limited" by another, transcendent world.

The futility of seeing the world in this way is stressed throughout the text. (In fact, the modern world would not be a "waste land" if it could be validly seen with Christian eyes; Eliot would not have the occasion to deplore the "heap of broken images.") The thwarted resurrection at the beginning and the end of "The Burial of the dead" attests to that futility. April is the "cruellest month" because the poet finds it impossible to partake in the re-awakening of Spring, and the "sprouting" of the "corpse" is very much in question. In *The Waste Land* there is, just as in Wittgenstein's and Kafka's thinking, a powerful urge to find redemption through a transcendent force, but Eliot, as the other two authors, realize that it is impossible to simply return to the traditional image of earth and heaven, of a vale of tears and a better world beyond. The thought of a transcendence is still there, but this transcendence is experienced as void.

Kafka: "The Hunter Gracchus"

This fragment of four pages (written around 1917, and never published during Kafka's lifetime) tells the story of a person who is ready and eager to go to the other world, but who finds himself condemned to remain on earth, presumably forever.

The story starts out, as most of Kafka's stories, with an exceedingly mundane scene:

Two boys sat on a wharf throwing dice. On the steps of a monument, in the shadow of a saber-brandishing hero, a man read a newspaper. A girl filled a bucket at the water fountain. A fruit vendor lay beside his merchandise and gazed across the lake. Through the open door and window of a tavern one could see two men drinking wine in the dim interior of the house.[36]

Into this scene sails a small boat, quietly, "and as if it were hovering above the water."[37] A seemingly dead person is carried out on a stretcher and brought to a nearby house. The mayor of the town, dressed ceremoniously in black, comes hurrying to the house. He finds the stranger in a room placed like a corpse lying in state. It is the Hunter Gracchus who, when they are left alone, tells the mayor his story.

Gracchus used to be a licensed hunter in the Black Forest. While hunting he fell into a ravine and bled to death. The boat, with which he arrived in the mayor's town, was to ferry him to the other world. But for some unspecified reason the boat failed to take the right turn, and thus never reached its destination. Since then Gracchus roamed the waters of the earth, desperately trying to find relief from his state of being neither alive nor truly dead. "And you do not have part in the other world?"[38] the mayor asks. Gracchus answers:

I am always on the grand stairway which leads to it. On this infinite flight of stairs I roam about, sometimes way up, and sometimes close to the bottom. Sometimes I find myself to the right, sometimes on the left, but I am always in motion. The hunter has turned into a butterfly.[39]

As Gracchus is neither alive nor dead, he is neither an inhabitant of the earth nor of the transcendence. He is lost between the worlds. He is lost in such a way, however, that the reality of his existence is his being in the world, while there are serious doubts about the nature and reality of the other world: "Whenever I make headway in moving upward, and I can already see above me the radiant gate, then I wake up in the old boat that has gotten stuck in some earthly water."[40] The vision of the gate to the other world, it seems, is only a dream. The only thing which is certain is the hunter's presence in the world.

Gracchus stresses that the pain of his state is not that he has died, but that something is "out of order." He was happy when he was alive, but he also welcomed death. If the one had followed the other in due course he would have no complaints. After having bled to death in the ravine, Gracchus joyfully "put on his shroud in the way a bride would put on her wedding dress."[41] It is the undefined nature of his present state which oppresses the hunter, his ontological homelessness.

The fragment ends with the mayor's question whether Gracchus intends to stay in his town, and the hunter's answer: "I am here, more I do not know, and more I cannot do. My boat is without a rudder. It drifts with the wind which blows in the deepest regions of death."[42] The unresolved situation of Gracchus is a fate about which he cannot do anything. He is in the world, but he does not belong to it. His movements are determined by forces which point to another world, but this other world cannot be reached anymore, may, in fact, be illusory. The fate of Gracchus represents a situation in which people long to be somewhere else, while being condemned to remain part of the world.

De Chirico: "The Nostalgia of the Infinite"

Giorgio de Chirico was born in 1888 in Greece, but most of his life he lived in Italy. He was a painter who drew significant inspiration from philosophy. Between 1911 and 1917 he painted the series of paintings which made him a classic of modern art, the works which he characterized as "pittura metafisica." During World War I he founded, with the ex-Futurist Carlo Carra, the "metaphysical school" of painting, which was to have a considerable influence on Surrealism. The surrealists revered and encouraged this part of de Chirico's work, but they were bitterly disappointed when the painter, after 1917, returned to more traditional and academic methods of painting. Like Eliot, de Chirico finally ceased to be a member of the avant-garde of Modern Art altogether.

"The Nostalgia of the Infinite" was painted in 1913-14. Although the major building is an actual structure in the city of Turino, it is dramatically taken out of its historical context and transplanted into a strange, vast landscape. It is not functionally connected with any other building in the picture. The most obvious feature of the structures in the picture is, in fact, their unrelatedness, and thus their startling strangeness. In the shade of the foreground stands a box or pedestal without recognizable purpose, from the right a shadow is cast on the open space from an unknown object, and in the portico, usually a fixture of public places in cities, stands in a landscape which is void of any social life. It is the absence of any historical and social context which renders the otherwise ordinary structures into the mystifying objects as which they appear in Chirico's painting. (In other paintings of the "metaphysical" series, this kind of mysteriousness is further heightened by the deliberate juxtaposition of things which functionally or historically do not belong together: a railroad track is adjacent to a Renaissance palace, a factory neighbors a medieval castle, a tailor's dummy sits like a traveller in a plaza, a marble statue is fitted with a leather or rubber ball for a head, etc.)

The dominant impression is emptiness and deadness. There are the outlines of two human figures, but these figures are dwarfed by the comparatively tall buildings and the vastness of the landscape. The sky is strikingly empty, and by painting the windows and door of the tower as black holes, Chirico emphasizes the desertedness of the scene. The flying pennants seem to indicate festivities and social life, but under the given circumstances they emphasize desolation rather than remedying it. They may, indeed, remind one of "the wind which blows in the deepest regions of death" mentioned earlier. This would go together with the almost total absence of organic life in de Chirico's "metaphysical" paintings, and the statement which he made about art: "The profound work will be drawn up by the artist from the furthest depths of his being; there no murmur of a brook, no song of a bird, no rustle of a leaf takes place."[43]

The above features constitute the basic method of de Chirico's "metaphysical" painting. It is a method by which the depicted objects are systematically denuded of the historical, social, and natural context in which they are usually found, and which thus reveals or emphasizes aspects of things which usually escape notice. This method, which de Chirico calls "metaphysical abstraction," exposes, as it were, a world beyond the ordinary world, thus justifying the painter's use of the philosophical term. In an essay "On Metaphysical Art" of 1919 de Chirico writes:

It is an axiomatic truth that madness is an inherent phenomenon in all profound artistic manifestations.

Schopenhauer defines the madman as a person who has lost his memory. It is an apt definition because, in fact, that which constitutes the logic of our normal acts and our normal life is a continuous rosary of recollections of relationships between things and ourselves and vice versa.

We can cite an example: I enter a room, I see a man sitting in an armchair, I note a bird cage with a canary hanging from the ceiling; I notice paintings on the wall and a bookcase with books. None of this startles nor astonishes me because a series of memories which are connected one to the other explains to me the logic of what I see. But let us suppose that for a moment, for reasons that remain unexplainable and quite beyond my will, the thread of this series is

Figure 1. Giorgio de Chirico, *The Nostalgia of the Infinite,* (1913-14)

broken. Who knows how I might see the seated man, the cage, the paintings, the bookcase! Who knows with what astonishment, what terror and possibly also with what pleasure and consolation I might view the scene. The scene, however, would not be changed; it is I who would see it from a different angle. Here we meet the metaphysical aspect of things. By deduction we might conclude that everything has two aspects: a normal one that we almost always see and which is seen by other people in general; the other, the spectral or metaphysical which can be seen only by rare individuals in moments of clairvoyance or metaphysical abstraction, just as certain bodies that exist within matter which cannot be penetrated by the sun's rays, appear only under the power of artificial light, under X-ray for example.[44]

The de-contextualization which is accomplished in the paintings by taking objects out of their historical, social, or natural environment is achieved in this experience of "metaphysical clairvoyance" by taking the moment of perception out of its normal time sequence (which bears some resemblance to Wittgenstein's looking at things *sub specie aeterni*) and thus rendering its content into a strange and fascinating phenomenon. What is common to the paintings and the reported experience is the stripping of the world of its normality, a normality which covers up the deeper aspects of things as with a veil. The purpose of art is to uncover, to get through to the hidden aspects of reality. And it is for this reason that art which accomplishes this can be called "metaphysical."

The "metaphysics" involved in de Chirico's paintings, then, is not one of the world beyond the world, but one of a peculiar aspect of the world of facts. It does not postulate a dualistic worldview as that, e.g., of Plato or Christianity, rather it deals with an expansion of the perception of the world of facts. Ontologically speaking, de Chirico is as much an immanentist as Wittgenstein. But as Wittgenstein, de Chirico felt an overwhelming desire to transcend the world, to depart from the world in search of a different abode. There is no other world beside the world of facts, but there is nevertheless the possibility of an exploratory departure from it. In the essay "Zeus as Explorer" of 1918, de Chirico expressed that feeling in this way:

Around me the international set of *modern* painters strove stupidly with over-exploited formulas and sterile systems.

I alone, in my squalid studio in the Rue Campagne-Premiere, began to glimpse the first shades of a more complete, more profound, more complicated art, or, in a word—at the risk of provoking a liver attack for a French critic—*more metaphysical.*

New land appeared on the horizon.

The great zinc-colored glove with frightening gilded fingernails, swinging over the door of the shop in the woeful currents of the urban afternoon, with its index finger pointing at the slabs of the sidewalk indicated to me the hermetic signs of a new melancholy . . .

I discovered new zodiacal signs on the ceiling as I watched its desperate flight, only to see it die in the depths of the room in the rectangle of the window which opened onto the mystery of the street.

The door half opened on the night of the hallway had the sepulchral solemnity of the stone rolled away from the empty tomb of the resurrected.

And the new annunciatory paintings took form.

Like autumn fruit we are by now ripe for the new metaphysic . . .

Under the sheds echoing with metallic shocks the signals are set at the sign for departure.

In the wall-boxes the bells ring.

It is time . . .

"Gentlemen, all aboard!"[45]

NOTES ON CHAPTER ONE

1. Ludwig Wittgenstein, "A Lecture on Ethics," *The Philosophical Review* 74 (1965): 9-10.

2. It is possible that Wittgenstein was influenced in this by certain remarks in Schopenhauer's *The World as Will and Representation* with which Wittgenstein was familiar. Schopenhauer repeatedly expressed the idea that religious statements convey truth allegorically: "A religion . . . has only the obligation to be true *sensu allegorico,* since it is destined for the innumerable multitude who, being incapable of investigating and thinking, would never grasp the profoundest and most difficult truths *sensu proprio.* Before the people truth cannot appear naked" (Arthur Schopenhauer, *The World as Will and Representation,* trans. E.F.J. Paynes, vol. 2 [New York: Dover]: 66). In this passage Schopenhauer assumes, to be sure, that religious language conveys something indirectly which can also be conveyed directly. Sometimes, however, he seems to conceive of religious language as something entirely without sense: "A symptom of this allegorical nature of religions is the mysteries, to be found perhaps in every religion, that is, *certain dogmas that cannot even be distinctly conceived,* much less literally true" (*Ibid.* My italics).

3. Wittgenstein, *Tractatus,* 4.024.

4. Revelation; of Saint John, 20:11-14.

5. Wittgenstein, "Lecture on Ethics," 7.

6. Norman Malcolm, *Ludwig Wittgenstein: A Memoir,* with a Biographical Sketch by George Henrik von Wright (London: Oxford University Press, 1958), 72.

7. Wittgenstein, *Tractatus,* 6.522.

8. Ludwig Wittgenstein, *Briefe an Ludwig von Ficker,* ed. Georg Henrik von Wright and Walter Methlagl(Salzburg: Otto Müller Verlag, 1969), 55, (my translation).

9. Wittgenstein, *Tractatus,* 6.45.

10. Ludwig Wittgenstein, *Notebooks 1914-1916,* ed. G.H. von Wright and G.E.M. Anscombe, with English trans. by G.E.M. Anscombe (Oxford: Blackwell, 1961), 7.10. 1916.(All quotations from the *Notebooks* will be identified by their date.)

11. *Ibid.*

12. Wittgenstein, "A Lecture on Ethics," 6.

13. *Ibid.,* 11-12.

14. Wittgenstein, *Notebooks 1914-1916,* 8.7, 1916.

15. Malcolm, *Ludwig Wittgenstein: A Memoir,* 20.

16. *Ibid.,* 72.

17. *Ibid.,* 20.

18. *Ibid.,* 72.

19. Engelmann, *Ludwig Wittgenstein. Briefe und Begegnungen,* 18-19, (my translation).

20. *Ibid.,* 59.

21. Wittgenstein, *Briefe an Ludwig von Ficker,* 28.

22. Bernhard Leitner, *The Architecture of Ludwig Wittgenstein. A Documentation,* with excerpts from the Family Recollections by Hermine Wittgenstein (Halifax: The Press of the Nova Scotia College of Arts and Design, 1973), 19.

23. Wittgenstein, *Briefe an Ludwig von Ficker,* 37.

24. Malcolm, *Ludwig Wittgenstein: A Memoir,* 10-11.

25. *Ibid.,* 25.

26. Friedrich Waismann, *Wittgenstein und der Wiener Kreis,* ed. B.F. McGuinness (Frankfurt a.M.: Suhrkamp Verlag, 1967), 117, (my translation).

27. Leo Tolstoy, *A Confession, The Gospel in Brief, and What I Believe,* trans. with an Introduction by A. Maude (London: Oxford University Press, 1967), 204.

28. *Ibid.,* 55.

29. Franz Kafka, "Von den Gleichnissen" in *Franz Kafka, Sämtliche, Erzählungen,* ed. Paul Raabe (Frankfurt a.M: Fischer Verlag, 1969), 359, (my translation). The piece has also been translated as "On Parables."

30. Cf. Ludwig Wittgenstein, *Lectures and Conversations on Aesthetics, Psychology and Religious Belief,* ed. Cyril Barrett (Oxford: B. Blackwell, 1966), 63, (hereafter cited as *Lectures and Conversations*).

31. Wittgenstein, *Briefe an Ludwig von Ficker,* 22.

32. Georg Trakl, *Die Dichtungen* (Salzburg: Otto Müller, 1938), 67, (my translation).

33. S. Bradley, R.C. Beathe, E.H. Long, eds., *The American Tradition in Literature,* vol. 2(New York: Norton, 1956, 1967), 1288-91. I have made use of the very helpful editors' notes.

34. *Ibid.,* 1288.

35. Bertrand Russell, *The Autobiography of Bertrand Russell. The Middle Years: 1914-1944* (New York: Bantam, 1968), 7.

36. Franz Kafka, "Der Jäger Gracchus" in Raabe, *Franz Kafka, Sämtliche Erzählungen,* 285, (my translation).

37. *Ibid.*

38. *Ibid.,* 287.
39. *Ibid.* The butterfly, on account of its having shed the body of the caterpillar, is in some cultures considered a symbol of resurrection, or of a soul that has transcended its body.
40. *Ibid.*
41. *Ibid.,* 288.
42. *Ibid.*
43. Giorgio de Chirico, quoted by Patrick Waldberg in *Surrealism* (New York and Toronto: Oxford University Press, 1965), 29.
44. Giorgio de Chirico, "On Metaphysical Art," trans. Joshua C. Taylor, in Herschel B. Chipp, *Theories of Modern Art. A Source Book by Artists and Critics,* (Berkeley and Los Angeles: University of California Press, 1968), 450.
45. *Ibid.,* 447.

CHAPTER TWO

THE EMERGENCE
OF THE
IRRATIONAL

THE EMERGENCE OF THE IRRATIONAL

A well-known paradigm of rational argument is the following syllogism:

> All men are mortal.
> Socrates is a man.
> Therefore, Socrates is mortal.

If it is granted that all men are mortal, and that Socrates is a man, then no rational being can possibly refute the conclusion that Socrates is mortal. The conclusion inexorably follows from the two premises. To admit the truth of the two premises and at the same time to deny the truth of the conclusion is tantamount to violating the most fundamental laws of thought; it amounts to not *thinking* at all.

It has always been a dream of philosophers to put politics and morality, as well as all other value systems, on a firm rational basis. If values would become a matter of reason, then questions of ethics, public policy, and other areas of human concern could be answered with the same certainty with which Socrates' mortality can be deduced from certain given premises. The organization of societies and individual conduct would not have to be left to the vagaries of feelings, private convictions, conventions, social pressures or even brute force, but could be settled on the basis of rational principles. The confusion and arbitrariness of unfounded opinions would be replaced by the clarity of logically derived rules to which every thinking person would have to agree. Wittgenstein refers to this philosophical ideal in his "Lecture on Ethics":

> Now let us see what we could mean by the expression 'The absolutely right road.' I think it would be the road which *everybody* on seeing it would, *with logical necessity,* have to go, or be ashamed for not going. And similarly the *absolute good,* if it is a desirable state of affairs, would be one which everybody, independently of his tastes and inclinations, would *necessarily* bring about or feel guilty for not bringing about.[1]

Reasoning does, in fact, often take place in moral or political discourse. Someone might say, for example: "You ought to vote for Party X." Someone else may ask: "Why should I do so?" And the first speaker may reply: "Because Party X supports the principle of equal rights for all citizens." This speaker does not simply demand that people vote for Party X, but buttresses his demand with a supporting reason.

The problem with this kind of reasoning is, of course, that it is not as compelling as the one displayed by the syllogism mentioned earlier. While the statement "Socrates is mortal" follows inexorably from the premises, the conclusion "You ought to vote for Party X" does not follow with logical necessity from the supporting reason. Even if one added further supporting reasons, someone may still refuse to draw the suggested conclusion without violating any laws of logic. For example:

Party X supports the principle of equal rights.

Party X works for the protection of the environment.

Therefore one ought to vote for Party X.

By adding further supporting reasons the suggested conclusion may eventually become extremely plausible to a great number of people, but a person who in the end refuses to draw the conclusion could by no means be accused of being irrational.

The only way in which the suggested conclusion could be made compelling for all rational beings is by constructing an argument of the kind exemplified by the first syllogism:

One should always vote for parties which support the principle of equal rights.

Party X supports the principle of equal rights.

Therefore one should vote for Party X.

In this argument the conclusion follows with logical necessity from the premises. That is, if one agrees with the two premises, then one could not possibly disagree with the conclusion without violating the laws of thinking. If everybody agreed on the two premises, the conclusion would have universal validity.

It is obvious, however, that this syllogistic maneuver does not accomplish what rationalistic philosophers have been hoping for, namely, to put value decisions on a rational basis. The original difficulty concerning the rational basis of value conclusions is simply shifted a step back. While the conclusion "You ought to vote for Party X" does, indeed, follow with logical necessity, the premise "One should always vote for parties which support the principle of equal rights" seems as arbitrary as the conclusion was before. People may or may not subscribe to it without in the least affecting their rationality.

Rationalistic philosophers would argue, of course, that the support for the principle of equal rights is not a matter of arbitrariness. They would hold that the principle can be defended on the basis of reason. Choosing from several possible supporting reasons, they may construe the following argument:

One should always vote for parties that promote the greatest happiness for the greatest number of people.

Parties that support the principle of equal rights promote the greatest happiness for the greatest number of people.

Therefore one should always vote for parties that support the principle of equal rights.

Again, the desired conclusion follows with logical necessity from the two premises, but the original difficulty reappears as well. Even if it is granted that the second premise be true, the first premise seems as arbitrary a conclusion as any rival position in morality or politics. There is certainly no universal agreement on whether the greatest happiness of the greatest number of people ought to be furthered, and thus a further argument needs to be constructed to support this stance.

At this point it becomes apparent that those who want to put value decisions on a firm rational basis by making value conclusions logically compelling, face rather dire prospects. For however far back they go in making value conclusions follow with logical necessity from any given premises, they always seem to be forced to introduce another value statement into the premises to achieve the desired result. They are faced, in other words, with an infinite regress. A solid starting point for the whole chain of reasoning seems to be hopelessly out of reach.

One hope for avoiding the infinite regress would be to find something like a "self-evident" truth. Thomas Jefferson, a rationalist and Enlightenment thinker, wrote in the *Declaration of Independence:*

We hold these truths to be self-evident, that all men are created equal, that they are endowed by their creator with certain inalienable rights, that among these are life, liberty, and the pursuit of happiness.

If any of these contentions could be accepted as self-evidently true, then it would indeed be possible to deduce other value statements with logical necessity, and by further deductions create an entire system of rules and institutions which could govern the life and conduct of people. The problem of finding a rational foundation for politics and morality would be solved. Unfortunately for the hopes of rationalistic philosophers, however, Jefferson's Enlightenment principles have not been found "self-evident." If they are to be accepted as universally valid, they will have to be supported by further compelling reasons, and thus be linked with the infinite regress. Reason, in the end, seems to be unable to bindingly settle questions of conduct and value.

The basic difficulty encountered by the rationalist philosopher is the seeming impossibility of deriving value conclusions from statements of fact. If value conclusions could be deduced from statements of facts, both the infinite regress and reliance on "self-evident" moral truths could be avoided. For the truth or falsity of statements of fact can be established independently of any personal or cultural preferences, and the rules of logic are equally objective. But the impossibility of deriving value conclusions without introducing questionable value statements into the premises seems to show that there is an unbridgeable gap between statements of fact and statements of value. And this "fact-value gap" implies that it is in principle impossible to ever derive universally valid values from the study of facts, that evaluations and rules of moral and political conduct will have to come from such non-rational sources as feelings, social pressures, traditions, and so forth. This is the view which Wittgenstein defended during the *Tractatus* period. In his "Lecture on Ethics" he writes:

> Now what I wish to contend is that, although all judgments of relative value can be shown to be mere statements of facts, no statements of fact can ever be, or imply, a judgment of absolute value. Let me explain this: Suppose one of you were an omniscient person and therefore knew all the movements of all the bodies in the world dead or alive and that he also knew all the states of mind of all human beings that ever lived, and suppose this man wrote all he knew in a big book, then this book would contain the whole description of the world; and what I

want to say is that this book would contain nothing that we would call an *ethical* judgment or anything that would logically imply such a judgment. It would of course contain all relative judgments of value and all true scientific propositions and in fact all true propositions that can be made. But all the facts described would, as it were, stand on the same level and in the same way all propositions stand on the same level. There are no propositions which, in any absolute sense, are sublime, important, or trivial. Now perhaps some of you will agree to that and be reminded of Hamlet's words: "Nothing is either good or bad, but thinking makes it so." But this again could lead to a misunderstanding. What Hamlet says seems to imply that good and bad, though not qualities of the world outside us, are attributes of our states of mind. But what I mean is that a state of mind, so far as we mean by that a fact which we can describe, is in no ethical sense good or bad. If for instance in our world-book we read the description of a murder with all its physical and psychological details, the mere description of these facts will contain nothing which we could call an *ethical* proposition. The murder will be on exactly the same level as any other event, for instance the falling of a stone. Certainly the reading of this description might cause us pain or rage or any other emotion, or we might read about the pain or rage caused by this murder in other people when they heard of it, but there will simply be facts, facts, and facts but no Ethics.[2]

The *Tractatus* makes the same points, although in an extremely condensed way:

All propositions are of equal value.
The sense of the world must lie outside the world. In the world everything is as it is, and everything happens as it does happen: *in* it no value exists. And if it did exist, it would have no value.
If there is any value that does have value, it must lie outside the whole sphere of what happens and is the case. For all that happens and is the case is accidental.
What makes it nonaccidental cannot lie *within* the world, since if it did it would itself be accidental. It must lie outside the world.
So too it is impossible for there to be propositions of ethics.
Propositions can express nothing that is higher.[3]

That all propositions are of equal value reflects, of course, that all facts are on the same level, that no fact is intrinsically more or less valuable than any other fact. This implies that nobody can learn from facts what ought to be done, how a good life is to be lived. If there is to be direction and purpose to a life, these have to come from outside of the sphere of facts. The meaning of life and the world are not embodied in what is the case. If a particular value should, as a matter of fact, govern the conduct of an individual or a society (as murder is, in fact, forbidden in most societies), then this is just another fact. That murder is so sanctioned is itself neither good or bad, but just part of the world.

That everything which is the case is "accidental" refers to section 6.3 of the *Tractatus:* "The exploration of logic means the exploration of *everything that is subject to law.* And outside logic everything is accidental." Since facts and values are not tied together by logic, their relationship is "accidental." If values are attached to facts, the attachment is arbitrary. It lacks the kind of (logical) necessity which would make evaluations binding for all rational beings.

There was an interesting disagreement between Wittgenstein and his friend Moritz Schlick which highlights the basic understanding which Wittgenstein had of the role of reason in matters of value. Schlick had written in his book *Questions of Ethics* that there are two conceptions of the good in theological ethics. According to the "more shallow" one, the good is good because God wills it. According to the more sophisticated conception, God wills the good because it is good. Wittgenstein disagreed with this representation.[4] In a conversation in 1930 Wittgenstein argued that the first of the two conceptions is more profound: good is that which God commands. For this conception cuts off every attempt to explain why the good is good, while the second, in reality a more shallow conception (the one preferred by Enlightenment philosophers), misconstrues the matter by suggesting that there can be an objective, independent justification for absolute values. The first conception states clearly that the nature of the good has nothing to do with facts, and that therefore it cannot be explained by reason.

It is clear, then, that Wittgenstein's early philosophy is significantly characterized by its opposition to the rationalism which has dominated the mainstream of Western thought since Plato, and which gained particular prominence in the philosophy of the Enlightenment. In this tradition the rational mind has always been understood as the center of a truly human existence. That is, among the various human faculties, reason has usually been considered as more important, essential, or valuable than emotions, instincts, drives, or the body. In a well developed individual, reason was to be in control of all other faculties, and in a civilized society human interaction was to be based on thoroughly rational principles.

Plato was the first Western philosopher to develop this model of human existence extensively and systematically, thereby setting the stage for all subsequent generations of thinkers. His basic view was essentially preserved throughout the Middle Ages in the form of Christian Theology, and Descartes, although in many ways opposed to the Medieval heritage, made the same reason-centered view the starting point of modern philosophy. By defining the innermost self as "thinking substance," Descartes reinforced the notion that any abandonment to the "lower" faculties amounts to an act of self-alienation for human beings. The Enlightenment (with the important exception of its maverick fellow-traveler Rousseau) still accepted this view, and much of the work done by the philosophers of this movement consists of attempts to show how reason can in fact be the sole basis and ultimate judge of all human affairs.

Of particular importance for the Enlightenment was the connection of reason and the ideal of self-determination. Such Enlightenment goals as personal autonomy and democratic government were mostly conceived as forms of self-rule by reason. Thus Kant wrote in his famous essay of 1784, "What is Enlightenment?":

Enlightenment is the release of human beings from their self-incurred tutelage. Tutelage is the inability to use one's reason without direction from someone else. This tutelage is self-incurred when its cause does not lie in the lack of reason, but in the lack of resolution and courage to use it without direction from someone else. *Sapere aude!* Have courage to use your own reason!—This is the motto of enlightenment.[5]

What made reason so appealing and important for Enlightenment thinkers was the potential universality of rational principles. The picture which these thinkers had of pre-Enlightenment humanity was one of helpless crowds divided by religious creeds, national boundaries, racial differences, classes, cultural traditions, or mutually incompatible legal systems, and they watched with dismay the almost incessant bloodshed and destruction which was caused by people's blind and deeply emotional allegiance to their respective particularities. Enlightenment philosophers expected no relief for humanity until people would begin to rely on the one faculty which they all have in common, the capacity to think. If people would be guided by the principles of reason, rather than by their traditions, feelings, social pressures, or brute force, they would not only embark on a course of progress, peace, cooperation, and general prosperity, but also realize their potential and become rational beings. This optimistic Enlightenment vision, together with the entire reason-oriented tradition of Western philosophy, had come under increasingly numerous attacks during the nineteenth century. As the failure of the Enlightenment to reach its goal, a peaceful, equitable, and democratically governed human society, became ever more apparent, the attacks became more caustic and widespread. Schopenhauer (whom Wittgenstein read with great interest as a young man) was one of the first anti-Enlightenment philosophers who gained prominence after the defeat of the Liberal revolutions of 1848. In his main work, *The World as Will and Representation,* he offered a model of human existence in which reason played only a minor role, while the real center of life was a blind and powerful Will which drives and motivates people in all of their enterprises. Nietzsche continued this theme in his writings, arguing time and again that the assumed supremacy of reason was as foolish an illusion as it was self-destructive, and that the entirety of rational Western civilization was not much more than a thin veneer over the basic bestiality of humankind. Kierkegaard, in a parallel development, criticized the futility of finding rational and universally valid foundations for ultimate value decisions, and he conceived of his "leap of faith" as the only way of coming to terms with one's existence. (Kierkegaard, too, was one of the philosophers whom Wittgenstein read, and of whose anti-rationalism he emphatically approved.[6]

The critical attitude toward (if not denunciation of) reason found expression not only in philosophy, but also in literature, journalism, and political reflections. It received powerful support from writers and creative artists such as Dostoyevsky, Wagner, Spencer, Bergson, and Unamuno. During the last few decades before the outbreak of World War I, anti-rationalism had almost become an intellectual fashion. In this sense Freud's discovery of the hitherto unacknowledged extent and power of the Unconscious did not occur in a vacuum (although the specifics of his theory were, of course, highly unpalatable for the majority of his contemporaries). Scores of writers and artists had already shed the belief in the basic rationality of human beings —a change which found expression in their often violent opposition to Western artistic traditions, in their growing interest in non-Western arts and cultures, and in their inventions of highly expressive forms of artistic creation. For a good many intellectuals of the time, the outbreak of World War I was likewise not an unexpected event, but the almost inevitable practical expression of the basic irrationality of man. The war was not even unwelcome by such thinkers, for it seemed to provide the long yearned-for opportunity to throw off the stifling restraints which a rationalistic civilization had put on people. Western civilization, in other words, was prepared for a general explosion of its assumptions and traditions. It was ready for a powerful emergence of the Irrational.

Although Wittgenstein abstained from any generalizing and programmatic statements, there is no doubt that his thinking was very close to the anti-rationalism of the period. This does not only fit the limitations of reason which he exposed in his writings, but also is in accord with the generally dark visions which he had concerning the state of the world. It is worthwhile emphasizing, however, that Wittgenstein's opposition to rationalism did not grow out of any hostility toward reason. He was not the kind of "Romantic" who finds his ideas and feelings disturbed by the "cold" inquiries of a sharp and disciplined intellect. On the contrary, Wittgenstein arrived at his anti-rationalistic conclusions because of his particularly exacting standards for rationality. By admitting as rational only those operations which conform to the laws of strict logical deductions, many forms of reasoning which were formerly accepted by thinkers as rational were excluded as deficient and unfit for doing the work of reason. Wittgenstein did not criticize reason from the basis of emotionalism or some other non-rational position, but exposed the failure of reason by invoking the strictest standards of reasoning. He did not attack rationalism from without, but exploded it from within.

Marinetti: "Against the Syllogisms"

Emilio Filippo Tommaso Marinetti was born in 1876. He pursued a literary career in France and Italy. In 1909 the Paris *Figaro* published his "Futurist Manifesto," which inspired modern artists and intellectuals in all European countries. When Mussolini rose to power, Marinctti aligned himself with the Fascists, thus considerably diminishing the general influence of the Futurist movement which he headed. He fought in the Abyssinian War and in World War II. He died in 1944.

Futurism was a violent rebellion against a culture which the rebels thought to be unbearably pretentious, stuffy, and debilitating. Futurism was opposed to tradition, reason, academism, and culture in general. It glorified modern technology, dynamism, the speed of modern machines, danger, and outright war. Some of the articles of the 1909 manifesto are:

Courage, audacity, revolt shall be the essential elements of our poetry . . .

We assert that the magnificence of the world has been enriched by a new beauty, the beauty of speed. A racing car with its bonnet draped in enormous pipes like fire-spitting serpents . . . a roaring racing car that goes like a machine gun is more beautiful than the Winged Victory of Samothrace . . .

We will glorify war, the only hygiene of the world—militarism, patriotism, the destructive gestures of anarchism, the great concepts of which men die, contempt of women.
We shall destroy the museums, libraries and academies of every kind, and will combat moralism, feminism and all vile opportunist utilitarianism.[7]

When Italy conquered Ethiopia in 1936, in a war in which the natives fought a modern war machine often with no other weapons than spears and shields, Marinetti wrote: "War is beautiful because it inaugurates the dreamed of metallization of the human body . . . War is beautiful because it creates new architectures, such as big tanks, the geometric fighter squadrons, the spirals of smoke rising from burning villages, and much more . . ."[8]

"Against the Syllogisms" was written before 1912.[9] It is a frontal attack on reason and logic, one of the cornerstones of the Enlightenment. In contrast to Wittgenstein, who in the *Tractatus* perfected the techniques of logic, and who showed the limits of reason as it were from within, Marinetti lambasts logic from without by ridiculing it in the name of irrational vitality:

AGAINST THE SYLLOGISMS

For they are your projectiles, powerful Ocean,
those petrified corpses which rest
at your bottom. The scholars say:
They are swollen, and they will all dissolve.
And the scholars have proved that.
But so what? Their scholarly wisdom is vain.
Look at their Syllogisms. They totter,
their white hair under their pointed magician's hats,
which disseminate derision towards the clouds!
Look at their formal conclusions: fat bodies

in X-forms which open and close
just as one likes, like those portable chairs
which for their convenience the hunters carry around.
In circles they dance, the Syllogisms,
always around the Truth, a maiden lovely and blue.
Dizzy, she closes her eyes.
Haha!
This tender Truth, like a very young girl,
immobilized by horror when touched by a scholar,
vanishes like a sorcerer's spook.
Only her golden veil remains in their clumsy clutches.
Haha!
Open up, you waves, open up
with a giant diamond laugh to the stars!
Explode with your dazzling laughter
the quiet of these sepulchral dungeons!
For look: Those Syllogisms, impotent,
whitehaired and shriveled, are licking the traces
of this ungraspable, ardently longed-for Truth!

The only thing I still believe in is
my towering Dream, bright as a lighthouse,
and his golden eye, big as the moon in the fall,
which roams the boundless depths of the night!

Marinetti's poetic ploy is to identify truth with a beautiful maiden, and
the means of logic and reason with impotent old men dressed in
ridiculous garb. Under those circumstances truth, of course, cannot be
gained by reason. It vanishes, leaving in the hands of reason only "her
golden veil," i.e., some externals of truth. Reason cannot get what reason
is really looking for.
    What gains truth are irrational forces, particularly the "dream."
Marinetti's argument here is that of the Romantics who had argued
earlier that by such means as feeling, dream, visions, or even drugs, more
insight into the truth of life can be gained than by ratiocination. (That the
truth in Marinetti's poem is "blue" may be an allusion to the legendary
Blue Flower of Romanticism.) Marinetti further allies the forces of
nature, the ocean, with the dream against reason: their power makes the
means of logic laughable. There is finally a strong sexual element
connected with the powers of the Irrational: not only are the syllogisms
"impotent," but the dream is also "high and bright like a lighthouse," a
characterization with a conspicuous phallic connotation.

Marinetti's poem clearly stands in the emerging tradition of anti-rationalism mentioned earlier. The images of the night contained in the last lines are reminiscent of the programmatic remarks in Nietzsche's "Ecstatic Song":

Pay attention, O humanity!
What does the depth of midnight say?
"I slept, I slept.—
I woke up from a deep dream:
The world is deep,
And deeper than the day had thought . . .[10]

What Nietzsche implies here is the same as what is expressed in Marinetti's poem, namely that day-consciousness, dominated by logic and reason, is not capable of grasping the full depth of the world. It implies that Rationalism is superficial (and the whole worldview of the Enlightenment shallow)—a thesis which Nietzsche had worked out more systematically in *The Birth of Tragedy* (1873). In this book Nietzsche argued that genuine art cannot come out of reason, but only out of ecstatic intoxication (represented by Dionysus) and dream (represented by Apollo). Dionysian intoxication reveals the ultimate nature of reality, its immeasurably profound and unredeemable horror. The Apollonian dream creates, as a reaction to this insight into the depth of the world, the world of beautiful appearance. Both powers are irrational. They are destroyed as soon as reason begins to dominate artistic production—as happened with the emergence of reason in the age of Socrates and classical Greek philosophy. It was the Rationalism of Socrates which, according to Nietzsche, led to the degeneration of Greek tragedy and art, and eventually to the debility of all of Western civilization.

Heym: "War"

Georg Heym was born in 1887 in Silesia. He studied law at the University of Berlin, but made literature his main pursuit. He was one of the initiators of literary Expressionism. His poems were regularly published in *Die Aktion,* a leading Expressionist journal with Anarchist and Futurist leanings. Heym's work deals extensively with the anti-idyllic features of the modern industrial and urban environment, and it contains recurring visions of apocalyptic wars and catastrophes. Heym was drowned in 1912 while attempting to rescue a skating companion who had broken through thin ice.

"War" was written in 1911-12. In the original German it is a rhyming poem.[11] (Like the poems by Baudelaire, which influenced his writing, Heym's poems tend to be modern in their vision, while remaining traditional in their external form.)

WAR

Up he rose, he who had slept so long.
Up he rose from vaults so deep.
Big and strange he's standing in the dusk.
And his blackened hand crushes the moon.

Far into the city's evening noise there falls
The chill and shadow of a foreign gloom.
The bustle of the market stops:
Stillness sets in. They look around. Nobody knows.

It haunts them in the narrow streets.
A question. But no answer. There a face is turning pale.
In the distance—tolling, trembling—bells.
Beards are quivering on pointed chins.

In the mountains he begins to dance,
And he yells: You, warriors, rise!
There is a roar when he his black head shakes,
And his necklace, made from human skulls.

Like a tower he stamps out the fading glow
Of the parting day, rivers are already red with blood.
Countless corpses lie among the reeds,
Covered white with death's strong birds.

He chases the fire across the fields into the night,
A dog, red, and with shrieks of many mouths.
Out of the dark emerges the black world of nights,
Its edges illuminated horribly by fiery peaks.

Thousands of flickering pointed caps
Are strewn across the gloomy plains.
And whatever flees along the swarming roads
Is pushed by him into the flaming, roaring woods.

And the flames devour forest after forest—
Yellow bats, clawed jaggedly into the leaves.
Beating like a charcoal-burner into trees
His giant poker, he makes the fire fiercely roar.

A city was submerged in yellow smoke,
And threw itself into the belly of the gulch.
But giantly above the smoldering debris
Stands he who turns three times his torch

Above the glow of storm-torn clouds
And the dead darkness of the chilling desert,
To scorch the night with his tremendous blaze,
And pour the burning pitch down on Gomorrah.

The poem was written at the end of a period which was characterized by unprecedented advances of a seemingly rational and science-oriented civilization, and half a century of almost uninterrupted peace. The poem's vision flew in the face of everything that Western humanity liked to think about itself.

To the majority of Europeans the Victorian Age looked in most ways like a realization of the ideals of the Enlightenment with its dreams of continuous progress, peace, and prosperity. Science, industry, and commerce flourished as never before, bringing not only an ever increasing degree of human control over the forces of nature, but also unheard of general standards of living. Rapid industrialization caused a massive migration of populations to urban centers. The growing cities created landscapes in which virtually everything was man-made. Mass transportation systems moved large numbers of people at high speeds, telecommunication created new ways of interaction, such things as electric street lights and indoor plumbing effected profound changes in traditional ways of life, and so forth. Standards of living became so high that even the lower classes began to feel that they had a stake in the existing socio-political system. Labor made significant gains with respect to income and political rights, and the formerly openly revolutionary socialist parties began to change into reformist organizations. The apparent stability of the situation in Europe made any thought of sudden or radical changes look like attacks of spleen or wild dreams. Stefan Zweig, a contemporary and compatriot of Ludwig Wittgenstein, describes the prevailing mood of the time in his autobiographical *The World of Yesterday:*

> The nineteenth century with its liberal idealism was honestly convinced to be on its way to 'the best of all possible worlds.' People looked contemptuously at former epochs with their wars, famines, and revolts; they saw them as a time when people simply had not yet come of age, when they lacked sufficient enlightenment. But today it was but a matter of decades before the last traces of evil and violence would be overcome. And this faith in inevitable and irreversible "Progress" had for this age the force of a religion; people began to believe in "Progress" more than in the Bible.[12]

During the last decade before World War I, the long period of apparent peace[13] began to change into an increasingly tense situation. The tension was largely caused by Germany's rise to a major industrial and military power in Europe. This newcomer nation (which was not founded as a political entity until 1871) came into increasingly frequent conflicts with the more established powers, England and France. After a number of crises, provoked by the less than skillful diplomacy of Kaiser Wilhelm II, a general war between Germany and the Hapsburg monarchy on the one side, and the alliance of England, France, and Russia on the other, became a disquieting possibility.

In 1911 the German navy sent a gunboat to Agadir in French Morocco. The ensuing international crisis created for the first time widespread concern, even panic. Liberal and left-wing newspapers began to warn of the catastrophe of a world war.[14] It was during this situation that Heym wrote "War."

War is represented in the poem as a dark force which suddenly rises from the depth where it had been forgotten for a long time. It is a force which disrupts everyday commerce, and which strikes terror into the hearts of the citizens of the civilized world. The image of war does not suggest the mechanized warfare which Marinetti glorified, and which World War I turned out to be, but rather the warrior of a "primitive" society, or a mythical war god. It represents the primal forces which civilized Europe had not acknowledged for a long time, and which were bound to erupt into the open against all efforts to repress them. (Freud's observations about the instinctive drives and their repression in civilization are relevant to the poem. The severity with which Victorian society repressed the open expression of sexuality and aggression may well explain the violence of the fantasies of those who rebelled against this culture.) The fact that the church bells are heard only in the distance (third stanza) may indicate that the institution which had brought civilization to Northern Europe, organized religion, has lost its control over the raw forces which it had once subdued.

The war dance starts in the mountains, i.e., away from the centers of civilization. But from there the destruction spreads, and finally sets the whole world aflame. The imagery of the sixth stanza is strongly reminiscent of certain pictures of hell created by the anti-classical painter Hieronymus Bosch (one of the older masters who was "re-discovered" by modern art). In the end, the apocalyptic destruction reaches "a city," i.e., the center of modern civilization: the primal force annihilates the work of culture.

In the situation in which it was written, "War" could have been (and has been) read as a prophetic warning of the impending world war. One could imagine the poet to be as horrified as the people at the beginning of the poem. But such a reading does not place enough emphasis on the fact that it is "Gomorrah" that is being destroyed, i.e., a civilization which has gone astray. An alternative reading, then, is that the destruction is a deserved one, that the poet sides, as it were, with the primal warrior[15] that destroys a civilization which has repressed everything which is original and true. In a sense, then, the poet is welcoming war. The civilization which is to perish is one of falseness, decadence, and lifelessness. And the apocalyptic fire is a vision of liberation, a destruction which has to come before any renewal.

Benn: "Threat"

Gottfried Benn was born in 1886 in Prussia. He studied medicine, and remained a practicing physician throughout his life. Between 1912 and 1917 he published poetry which in many ways was expressionistic. But Benn had relatively few contacts with Expressionism as a movement. While the latter was predominantly inclined toward humanism and the Left, Benn's writings were nihilistic, opposed to the Enlightenment, and increasingly inspired by a view of art according to which the discipline of artistic form is the only substantial element in an otherwise hopelessly chaotic and degenerate world. His nihilistic views made him at least tolerant of Fascism when Hitler assumed power in 1933. As the regime pressed its anti-modernistic stance in the arts, however, Benn became weary of the Nazis. He avoided frictions with the authorities by joining the army medical corps in 1935. After the war Benn returned to his private practice of medicine. He died in Berlin in 1956.

The following poem is part of Benn's early work; it was written in 1913 as part of a longer poem:[16]

THREAT

But know this:
I live animal days. I am a water hour.
In the evening my lid grows tired like the woods or the sky.
My love knows only very few words:
It is so wonderful close to your blood.

The poem stands for a similar kind of irrationalism as that of Heym's poem, but it expresses this attitude in a more intimate context. In spite of its title, Benn's text is a love poem. It expresses tenderness toward a woman, while formulating an implicit threat to her humanity.

By stating "I live animal days" the poet rejects everything which distinguishes humans from animals: reason, language, rational self-control, art, the sublimation of "lower" drives, etc. He rejects not only the stiltedness and hypocrisy of a particular culture, the Victorianism of the pre-World War I period, but human civilization in any form. All specifically human ways of life are rejected in favor of a return to nature, to noncivilized forms of existence. "I am a water hour" indicates the kind of timelessness which Benn has in mind: Water is characterized by its shapelessness, its ability to exist in many forms and shapes. The time of the "animal days" is equally flexible, unstructured. The poet thus opposes the rigid time structure which civilization has imposed on people and other forms of life. The "tyranny of the clock," which makes millions of people wake up, work, coordinate their activities with machines, take their breaks, make love, socialize, or go back to sleep at the same time, is rejected in favor of a way of life which is in harmony with "the woods or the sky." The structuredness of the contemporary technological civilization is to be replaced not just by a pre-industrial, more leisurely, culture, but by a state of nature which is untouched by any human intervention.

The opposition to civilization in the poem is reflected in its deliberate artlessness. It is composed of simple statements which are added together. There is no rhyme scheme or rhythmic pattern. Its shortness supports what it says: "My love knows only few words," for words are already too civilized. Language is to give way to mere actions and gestures.

The poet is not interested in the addressed woman as a person, i.e., as a being with mind, character, goals, or social involvements. He is attracted to her "blood," the substance which symbolizes anonymous, impersonal life. The relationship which the poet envisions is not one between identifiable and conscious, let alone sophisticated, individuals, but between forces of nature. An individual is not drawn to another individual, but blood to blood. It is a process of nature which functions far beneath the institutions and conventions of a civilization which in Benn's eyes is vain and futile.

Benn's anti-rationalism goes farther than that of Heym or other Expressionists. He does not simply oppose a civilization which values reason higher than emotions, but condemns civilization altogether. Benn's poetic imagination turns evolution back to a point where life is reduced to its most simple forms: life is bearable only in its most archaic manifestations. In another poem Benn writes: "O if we could be our most ancient ancestors: lumps of slime in a warm bog!"[17] If it is only at this level that a being can find peace, any *human* relationship is inevitably a form of self-alienation. A lover who speaks to a woman from such a depth is a stranger in human society, and what he says is by necessity a "threat" to human individuals as persons.

Ball: "Dirge"

Hugo Ball was born at Pirmasens, Germany in 1886. He studied philosophy without, however, finishing his Ph.D. dissertation on Nietzsche. Before World War I he published poetry and several plays. Making a living as a director and critic in Munich and Berlin, he became thoroughly acquainted with the avant-garde in theatre, literature, and art. After the outbreak of the war he soon became profoundly disillusioned with a culture which permitted and sustained the carnage at the fronts. In 1915 he moved to Switzerland. In Zurich, together with such international expatriates as Tristan Tzara, Marcel Janco, and Hans Arp, he founded the Cabaret Voltaire and the Dada movement. In 1917 he left Dadaism (and Modern Art in general), and eventually converted to Catholicism. He died in 1927.

"Dirge"[18] was one of the "poems without words" which Ball wrote in April 1916, and which he presented at the Cabaret Voltaire.

DIRGE

ombula
take
bitdli
solunkola
tabla tokta tokta takabla
taka tak
Babula m 'balam
tak tru—ü
wo—um
biba bimbel
o   kla   o   auw
kla o auwa
la—auma
o   kla   o   ü
la   o auma
klinga—o—e—auwa
ome   o-auwa
klinga   inga   M ao—Auwa
omba dij omuff pomo—auwa
tru—ü
tro-u-ü   o-a-o-ü
mo-auwa
gomun guma   zangaga   gago   blagaga
szagaglugi   m   ba-o-auma
szaga   szago
szaga la m 'blama
bschigi bschigo
bschigi bschigi
bschiggo   bschiggo
goggo   goggo
ogoggo
a—o—auma

The "poem without words" represents in literature what Kandinsky's abstract pictures are in painting. Kandinsky (whom Ball knew personally from his days in Munich) was the first painter who used colors, lines, and surfaces not as means to depict objects, but rather as means to influence the viewer directly, without engaging his or her intellectual faculties. The visual means of painting were to transmit emotions from the artist to the perceiver not via some "narrative" content, which would have to be processed by the intellect, but merely by their own structure and combination. Painting was to function as much as possible as music. In the same way Ball uses the audible means of language, sounds and rhythm, not as a means to transmit a narration or other kinds of meaning, but as means to activate the non-rational faculties of his listeners. They constitute a kind of music.

Thus the text is not only without literal meaning, but also without sentences or other kinds of grammatical structure. And its "words" are, strictly speaking, not words, but sounds. When "spoken" they resemble the hypnotic incantations of a shaman or some other priest, evoking the feeling of a situation rather than delivering a description. In bypassing the rational faculties, they allow a concentration on the emotive qualities of sound which is hardly possible in normal language.

Ball was very conscious of what he and his friends were doing. (It is one of the oddities of modern irrationalism that it was always accompanied by elaborate rational explanations and justifications.) In his journal of the Zurich Dada period he writes on June 18, 1916:

> We have now driven the plasticity of the word to the point where it can scarcely be equaled. We achieved this at the expense of the rational, logically constructed sentence, and also by abandoning documentary work (which is possible only by means of a time-consuming grouping of sentences in logically ordered syntax).[19]

Ball was also well aware of the attempts of other writers to "liberate" words from the fetters of rationalism. His own "poems without words" he saw as a further development of Marinetti's *Parole in Liberta* (Words in Freedom) of 1914:

> With the sentence having given way to the word, the circle around Marinetti began resolutely with "parole in liberta." They took the word out of the sentence frame (the world image) that had been thoughtlessly and automatically assigned to it, nourished the emaciated

big-city vocables with light and air, and gave them back their warmth, emotion, and their original untroubled freedom. We others went a step further. We tried to give the isolated vocables the fullness of an oath, the glow of a star. And curiously enough, the magically inspired vocables conceived and gave birth to a new sentence that was not limited and confined by any conventional meaning. Touching lightly on a hundred ideas at the same time without naming them, this sentence made it possible to hear the innately playful, but hidden, irrational character of the listener; it awakened and strengthened the lowest strata of memory. Our experiments touched on areas of philosophy and of life that our environment—so rational and so precocious—scarcely let us dream of.[20]

Finally, Ball understood the emergence of the irrational as one of the fundamental features of all of Modern Art, as a goal in the light of which the accomplishments of modern artists can be evaluated:

Pictures circa 1913. A new life was expressing itself in painting more than in any other art. It was the dawn of a visionary advent. At Goltz's gallery I saw pictures by Heuser, Meidneer, Rousseau, and Jawlensky. They illustrated the maxim *Primum videre, deinde philosophari* [First see, then philosophize]. They had achieved total expression of life without a detour through the intellect. The intellect was eliminated because it represented a wicked world.[21]

Schmidt-Rotluff: "Nude"

Karl Schmidt-Rotluff was born in 1884 in Saxony. In 1905 he went to Dresden to study architecture. There he joined the group of Expressionist painters known as "Die Brücke." In 1911 he moved to Berlin. In the 1920s his style softened considerably, becoming more fit for general consumption. Nevertheless, his style remained modernistic enough to be classified as "degenerate" by the Nazi authorities, after they assumed power in 1933. After World War II Schmidt-Rotluff taught at the Art Academy in Berlin. He died in 1976.

"Die Brücke" (The Bridge) was a rather close circle of friends who formed an important group of modernist painters between 1905 and 1910. The best known members were Kirchner, Heckel, Nolde, Muller, Pechstein, and Schmidt-Rotluff. They first worked in Dresden, where most of them were students at the art academy, and later in Berlin. Most of them were architects rather than painters. Their lack of formal training in painting they saw as an asset, as it made it easier for them to avoid the academism against which they rebelled. The major influence on them was Edward Munch, who had spent some time in Germany. They also informed themselves eagerly about the Modern Art rebellions which were evolving in Paris. Their common conviction was that art is to express the primal feelings within, rather than to influence artistic production from without by such means as aesthetic dogmas, rules, or conventions. Out of this common conviction they created a style which is characterized by extremely bold (usually primary) colors, simplified forms, and very rough technique.

Schmidt-Rotluff's "Nude" is a typical example of the Expressionists' revolt against rationalism and a repressive culture seemingly shaped by belief in reason. That nudes were a preferred subject of the Brücke artists is not coincidental. Nakedness expresses an opposition to covering up, to civilization, and to artificial conventions. It represents human beings in a state of nature, in a state which is more original than the manipulated conditions of culture. It is closer to the primal paradise which Expressionists tried to recapture.

Nudes were, of course, a regular item even of academic art. But the unabashed sexuality of the human body (together with the Expressionists' innovative style) created such an uproar among the public, that the police closed down Brücke exhibits on more than one occasion. This reaction on the part of official culture could, of course, only confirm the artists' belief that they had struck a raw nerve, that the dominant civilization was indeed committed to the repression of everything which is natural and true.

Because of their interest in primal originality, Brücke artists had a lively interest in "primitive" art, an interest which was inspired by Gaugin's turn to Oceanic art, and a similar interest in African sculpture on the part of Braque and Picasso. Frequent visits to the Anthropology Museum were a regular feature of Brücke activities. The Expressionists' interest in "primitive" art is reflected in Schmidt-Rotluff's woodcut not only by the presence of an Oceanic artifact in the background, but also by the mask-like appearance of the woman's face. The artist's interest was obviously not to give a realistic representation of a woman, but to create a figure which is strongly reminiscent of the magic of ritual statues and other sacred objects of primitive cultures.

One of the art forms particularly cultivated by the Brücke Expressionists

Figure 2. Karl Schmidt-Rotluff, *Nude*, (19 ?)

was the woodcut. They exploited its possibility of rough texture, hard outlines, and jagged surfaces. The fact that mistakes cannot be corrected on a cut block was welcomed by them, since it forces the artist to entirely rely on his spontaneity. And the vigorous distortions of the represented subject matters, which the medium encourages, accorded well with their stylistic intentions, which were formed by their will to express rather than represent faithfully and in tranquility.

The reduction of rational control is emphasized by Expressionists not only in their finished works, but also in the nature of their creative process. Artistic creation was conceived as a state of Dionysian inspiration, of frenzied ecstasy. Pechstein once described the process of his work in the following way: "Work! Intoxication! Smash the brain! Chew, eat, gobble down, rummage! Lustful pain of birth! Crashing of the paint brush. Would be wonderful to smash right through the canvas!" By shifting the emphasis from the finished product to the process of creation (thus making the work a mere document of something more alive and immediate), the Brücke Expressionists moved yet closer to what is central to their art, the vibrant presence of the unadulterated forces of life, the forces which were to consume everything structured, ossified, and dead.

NOTES ON CHAPTER TWO

1. Wittgenstein, "A Lecture on Ethics", 7, (emphases in the original).
2. *Ibid.,* 6-7.
3. Wittgenstein, *Tractatus,* 6.4 - 6.42.
4. Freidrich Waismann, *Ludwig Wittgenstein und der Wiener Kreis,* Gespräche, aufgezeichnet von Friedrich Waismann (Frankfurt a.M.: Suhrkamp Verlag, 1967), 115.
5. Immanuel Kant, *Foundations of the Metaphysics of Morals,* trans. L.W. Beck (Indianapolis: Bobbs-Merrill, 1959), 85.
6. Malcolm, *Ludwig Wittgenstein. A Memoir,* 71.
7. Quoted in Trewin Copplestone, *Modern Art Movements* (London, New York, Sydney, Toronto: Hamlyn, 1962), 24.
8. Quoted by Walter Benjamin, "Das Kunstwerk im Zeitalter seiner technischen Reproduzierbarkeit," in *Schriften,* vol. 1 (Frankfurt: Suhrkamp Verlag, 1955), 395-96, (my translation).
9. The only text available to me is a German translation of Marinetti's poem: "Gegen die Syllogismen," in F[ilippo] T[ommaso] Marinetti, *Futuristische Dichtungen,* autorisierte Übertragungen von Elfe Hudwiger (Berlin: A.R. Mayer, 1912), 7-8, (my translation from German into English).
10. Freidrich Nietzsche, "Das Trunkene Lied," in *The Penguin Book of German Verse* (Baltimore: Penguin, 1957), 375, (my translation).
11. Georg Heym, "Der Krieg," *ibid.,* 435, (my translation).
12. Stefan Zweig, *Die Welt von Gestern. Erinnerungen eines Europäers* (Frankfurt: Suhrkamp, 1949), 16, (my translation).
13. The ruthless conquest of Alsace-Lorraine by Germany in the war of 1870-71, the bloody repression of the Paris Commune by the Versailles government in 1871, and several brutal colonial wars made the more observant Victorians somewhat wary of calling the epoch "peaceful."
14. I have made use of the outstanding documentation concerning Heym's "War" presented in G. Dammann, K.L. Schneider, and J. Schoberl, eds. *Georg Heims Gedicht "Der Krieg"* (Heidelberg: C. Winter, 1978).
15. *Ibid.,* 49.
16. Gottfried Benn, *Gesammelte Werke in vier Bänden,* ed. Dieter Wellershoff, vol. 3 (Wiesbaden: Limes, 1960), 23.
17. *Ibid.,* 56.
18. Hugo Ball, *Gesammelte Gedichte* (Zürich: Arche, 1963), 26.

19. Hugo Ball: *Flight Out of Time: A Dada Diary,* ed. John Elderfield, trans. Ann Raimes (New York: Viking, 1974), 67.

20. *Ibid.,* 68.

21. *Ibid.,* 5.

CHAPTER THREE

THE DISINTEGRATION
OF REALITY

THE DISINTEGRATION OF REALITY

It is instructive to start the analysis of Wittgenstein's characterization of reality in the *Tractatus* with a look at that part of logic which is known as the "elementary calculus of propositions," and which is used and developed extensively in Wittgenstein's book. This calculus is essentially a set of rules which prescribe how propositions (i.e., descriptive sentences such as "The water is clear") can be combined with each other to form more complex propositions. Thus, the two elementary propositions "Agricultural production is mechanized" and "People migrate to the cities" can be combined into the more complex proposition "If agricultural production is mechanized, then people migrate to the cities." The expression "if . . . then," by means of which the two elementary propositions are combined, is called a "logical connective" or a "logical constant." (Wittgenstein refers to these "logical connectives" as "logical *constants*," whereas conventional mathematics would refer to a "connective" as an "operator," while using the word "constant" in a different connotation.) In analogy to mathematical expressions, the connectives are treated as constants, while the propositions are treated as the corresponding variables.

In the calculus employed by Wittgenstein there are four basic connectives. Besides "if . . . then" there are "and," "or," and "not." Thus, besides the complex proposition mentioned above one can also form the following ones: "Agricultural production is mechanized *and* people migrate to the cities," "Agricultural production is mechanized *or* people migrate to the cities," and "It is *not* the case that agricultural production is mechanized." (The negation of any elementary proposition is a complex proposition.)

To facilitate statements in the calculus, propositions are replaced by the lower case letters p, q, r, s, etc. Thus, the complex propositions just mentioned are written as:

$$\text{if} \quad p \text{ then } q$$
$$p \text{ and } q$$
$$p \text{ or } \quad q$$
$$\text{not} \quad p$$

For the sake of convenience, the logical constants are also replaced by symbols. Different logicians use different symbols, but Wittgenstein (following Russell's and Whitehead's *Principia Mathematica*) uses the following (in the above order):

$$p \supset q$$
$$p \cdot q$$
$$p \vee q$$
$$\sim p$$

As the elementary propositions p and q can be combined into such complex propositions as p⊃q, so the complex propositions can be combined, with the help of suitable brackets and parentheses, into still more complex statements. For example:

$$[(p \supset q) \cdot p] \supset q$$

In terms of the above examples, this statement reads: "If agricultural production is mechanized, people migrate to the cities. Agricultural production is mechanized. Therefore, people would migrate to the cities." Statements of even greater complexity can be constructed in this manner. It is one of the major theses of the *Tractatus* that the entirety of "meaningful language" is ultimately made up of elementary propositions and their various combinations, related by logical connectives. Or, to put the same thing differently, the complex propositions which constitute language can ultimately all be analyzed into so many elementary propositions and a number of "ands," "ors," "if . . . thens," and "nots." As the truth or falsity of a complex proposition depends ultimately on the truth or falsity of the elementary propositions of which it is composed, complex propositions are called "truth-functions" of elementary propositions.[1] And one of the major purposes of the propositional calculus is to provide a mechanical method by which one can determine the truth or falsity of very complex propositions through analyzing them into their elementary components.[2]

So far the symbolic rendering of ordinary propositions does not appear to be more than the translation of one language (ordinary English) into another (the propositional calculus). But this appearance is deceptive. As in many other cases, things become lost or changed in the translation. The translation of the ordinary "and" into the "." of the calculus does, in fact, involve a significant change of meaning, as does the translation of the other connectives. A closer look at these changes will reveal important aspects of Wittgenstein's view of the world.

In the language of the calculus, the complex proposition "Agricultural production is mechanized, and people migrate to the cities" simply asserts that the two elementary propositions taken together are true— just as the complex proposition "Agricultural production is mechanized, and Socrates was executed in Athens." In neither case is anything said about the connection between the events in question. The events may or may not have anything to do with each other, it does not make any difference for the conjunction of the calculus.

The same is true with p⊃q, and here the divergence of the calculus from ordinary English is even more striking. When one ordinarily says "If agricultural production is mechanized, then people migrate to the cities," then one implies, of course, that the one event follows from the other, that there is some kind of causal relation between the two. But again, for the logician's purpose, it is perfectly all right to say something like "If agricultural production is mechanized, then Cuba is an island." For p⊃q asserts nothing except that if p is true, then q is also true. It does not assert any kind of connection between the events described by p and q. The connection effected by ⊃, again, is not one between facts or events, but between propositions.

This becomes clearer if one reformulates p⊃q. Since p⊃q says that if p is true, then q is also true, it says nothing else than that it is not the case that p is true and q is false. This latter formulation is symbolized as ~(p.~q). Since the two formulations say the same thing, they can be used in lieu of each other. The new formulation, however, does not use the suggestive expression "if . . . then," and therefore has the advantage of diminishing the temptation to assume a causal relationship where none is implied. It helps one to remember, in other words, that p⊃q deals only with the truth or falsity of p and q, and not with what they describe, or with the actual relation between the described events.

To underline this crucial point still further one can point to the fact that within the calculus of propositions all logical connectives can be replaced by each other according to some fixed rules. In the preceding paragraph it was pointed out that "if . . . then" can be replaced by a combination of "not" and "and." In a similar way "and" can be replaced by a combination of "not" and "or." Thus, the expression p.q is logically equivalent to the expression ~(~pv~q). Such substitutions show that none of the connectives is really essential for saying what is stated in complex propositions, and that for that reason they cannot signify any specific connections between facts or events.[3]

Wittgenstein states this understanding of the nature of logical connectives (or "constants") in the *Tractatus* on several occasions:

My basic idea is that 'logical constants' do not represent anything.[4]

But that the sign 'p' and '~p' can say the same thing [i.e., depict the same state of affairs] is important. For it shows that nothing in reality corresponds to the sign '~'.[5]

And if there were something called '~', then '~~p' would say something else than 'p'.[6]

The last remark presupposes that "p" and "~~p" are logically equivalent, that an affirmation amounts to the same as a double negation. ("It is raining" says the same thing as "It is not the case that it is not raining.") But this means that only the proposition depicts something of the world, while negations are operations which pertain only to the level of language or symbolism.

It is not necessary here to go further into the details of the propositional calculus, for what is important for Wittgenstein's view of the world is already visible. It can be stated as follows. (1) In the calculus, by conjoining factual propositions, it is possible to juxtapose facts which in ordinary reality have nothing to do with each other ("If agricultural production is mechanized, then Socrates was executed in Athens"). (2) Connections which may actually exist in reality are not conveyed in the language of the calculus. (The proposition "If agricultural production is mechanized then people migrate to the cities" does not say what at first sight it seems to say, namely that the one event occurs because of the other.) This means that the world as perceived ordinarily, and as conveyed in ordinary discourse, represents a different order of facts than the world conveyed by the calculus of propositions: what can be combined in one, cannot be combined in the other, and vice versa. While in ordinary discourse, the concept of causality, for example, is understood, in the calculus it does not exist. The two languages do not represent the same world in different media, but represent, as it were, two different realities.

The essential feature of the reality represented by the calculus is the basic and pervasive disconnectedness of all facts. As has been pointed out, the description of the world in terms of the calculus does not convey any of the connections which may exist in ordinary reality. And the combination of facts which are possible in the medium of the calculus, such as the mechanization of agriculture and Socrates' execution, are such that the basic unrelatedness (or mutual isolation) of facts is only highlighted. For the fact that in the calculus everything can be combined with everything else with equal validity demonstrates that there is no inherent connection between facts, that there is no inherent order which structures the world in a coherent way. The reality represented by the calculus of propositions is a world of randomly combined, but basically isolated facts. In comparison with the cohesiveness of ordinary reality, it is profoundly chaotic.

This is not contradicted by Wittgenstein's emphasis of the order of the "*logical* space" in which the world exists. In section 1.13 Wittgenstein says: "The facts in *logical* space are the world," i.e., the facts are subject to the laws of logic. But it is exactly Wittgenstein's emphasis of the *logical* order which permits the disregard for the much more restrictive order of ordinary reality, which is not only subject to the laws of logic, but also to those of causality, gravity, and so forth. In section 6.375 Wittgenstein says: "Just as the only necessity that exists is *logical* necessity, so too the only impossibility that exists is *logical* impossibility.[7] In other words, everything is allowed which does not violate the laws of logic. And since the juxtaposition of the mechanization of agriculture and the execution of Socrates, as senseless as it is with respect to ordinary reality, does not go against the rules of the calculus, it is a permissible combination. In spite of the prevailing order of logic, then, the world of the calculus of propositions is a chaos. It is the kind of reality which corresponds to that envisioned by Lautreamont and the Surrealists when they invoked their famous encounter of "an umbrella and a sewing machine on an operating table."

Ordinarily, logicians do not draw any ontological conclusions from their calculi, and they certainly do not go so far as to talk about "different realities." A calculus, after all, is nothing but a set of rules for the manipulation of certain symbols. In specific cases, a calculus can be used to represent certain aspects of reality in the way in which mathematical equations can be used to represent the orbits of planets or price fluctuations on the stock market, but the suitability of a calculus for such tasks has to be determined from case to case. Basically a calculus is a system which is defined in terms of its own axioms, and thus independently of reality.

In the *Tractatus,* however, the calculus of propositions (as all of logic) plays a much more eminent role. In this work logic is not just a number of arbitrarily defined systems *in* the world, but the underlying order *of* the world. In 6.13 Wittgenstein says: "Logic is not a doctrine, but a mirror-image of the world.—Logic is transcendental." The word "transcendental" is used here in the Kantian sense. That logic is transcendental means that one necessarily perceives the world as something which is subject to the laws of logic, that the basic structure of reality is identical with the order of logic. The order of facts as represented by the language of the propositional calculus, therefore, is not just one order among others that are possible, but it is *the* order of the world. The basic disconnectedness of all facts is, therefore, the true state of the world. Ordinary perception, and whatever is conveyed by ordinary language, can only give a distorted image of reality. The connections which they suggest are not real. A philosophical view of the world recognizes them as illusions.

The world as a conglomerate of disconnected facts is a conception which recurs throughout the *Tractatus:*

The world divides into facts.[8]

Anything can be the case or not be the case, while everything else remains the same.[9]

States of affairs are independent of each other.[10]

From the existence or non-existence of one state of affairs one cannot infer the existence or non-existence of another.[11]

There is no possible way of making an inference from the existence of one situation to the existence of another, entirely different situation.[12]

It may not be entirely unimportant that Wittgenstein says in 1.2: "Die Welt *zerfällt* in Tatsachen." It is usually translated as "The world *divides* into facts." This translation is correct, but "zerfällt" is a much more expressive word than "divides." It literally means "falls apart," or "disintegrates," thus connoting an image of the world which stresses the world's lack of cohesion, its basic state of entropy. "Die Welt zerfällt in Tatsachen," in other words, may be taken literally, for it conveys well Wittgenstein's perception of reality. It expresses the, as it were, disillusioned worldview of the Tractarian philosopher.

One of the most important implications of this view of the world is Wittgenstein's denial of the existence of causality. Here the divergence of his philosophical worldview from the ordinary perception of reality is most obvious. In sections 5.136 and 5.1361 he writes (continuing the line of thought of the last quotation given above):

> There is no causal nexus to justify such an inference.—We *cannot* infer the events of the future from those of the present.—Belief in the causal nexus is a *superstition*.[13]

According to the ordinary (i.e., *nonphilosophical*) understanding of things the mechanization of agriculture, e.g., is the *cause* of the migration of large numbers of people to the urban centers, because mechanization eliminates traditional occupations and livelihoods. And this urbanization, in turn, is the *cause* of the disappearance of older values, expectations, and behavior patterns because it implies a break-up of traditional communities, etc. In the nonphilosophical understanding of things, facts and events hang together, they follow each other in a way which is often predictable. If certain things are the case, certain other things are said to follow with necessity. It is this necessity with which events are said to follow each other which Wittgenstein denounces as a "superstition."

The lack of necessary connections between facts can be perceived by comparing the relation between facts to the logical relation between premises and conclusions:

> There is no compulsion which makes one thing happen because something else happened.[14]

> The exploration of logic is the exploration of everything which is subject to law. And outside of logic everything is accidental.[15]

If it is true that all men are mortal, and that Socrates is a man, then it follows with necessity that Socrates is mortal. The urbanization of society, by contrast, does not follow with the same necessity from the mechanization of agriculture. One can admit to the fact (or facts) that men are replaced by machines, that no new jobs are opening up in the countryside, etc., and still deny that people will migrate to the cities, without committing a *logical* mistake. And this lack of a necessary connection between mechanization and urbanization is not just due to the complexity of the situation which could allow for intervening factors. Even very simple events, such as the hitting of a ball and the ball's ensuing movement, are not related with *logical* necessity, according to the

Tractatus. If the ball is hit, it does not follow logically that the ball will move. It is imaginable that the ball will stay in its place after the impact. If it does move, its movement occurs "accidentally," i.e., without necessity. A special case of the disconnectedness of facts is the disconnectedness of the acts of will from what is willed:

The world is independent of my will.[16]

Even if all that we wish for were to happen, still this would be a favor granted by fate, so to speak: for there is no *logical* connection between the will and the world, which would guarantee it, and the supposed physical connection itself is surely not something that we could will.[17]

That the world is independent of my will may seem a trivial observation, as obviously not everything that one wills comes about. The cases which are interesting for Wittgenstein's conception of the world are those where one is successful in achieving what one wills. In such cases, the will could be seen as the cause of what happens. But again, as the connection between the hitting of a ball and the ball's movement is "accidental," so is that between the act of will and any ensuing event. No matter how realistic the object of one's will may be, it is in principle unpredictable what the outcome of one's willing will be. Thus, as all facts are essentially isolated from each other, so is the willing self isolated from the facts of the world. The ontological fragmentation which characterizes the world also characterizes the relation of the willing self to the world.

To appreciate the significance of Wittgenstein's characterization of reality as a conglomerate of disconnected facts, it is helpful to contrast it with the kind of conception to which it is diametrically opposed. Marx's analysis of history and society is a case in point. It is clear that a Marxist description of such events as the mechanization of agriculture and the urbanization of society will not represent them as isolated facts, but will emphasize and explore their connection with their historical context and other events, making extensive use of the category of cause and effect. It is, indeed, one of the fundamental tenets of Marxism that facts are not describable, let alone explainable, except by seeing them as parts of larger developments. History, for Marx, was not an unstructured sequence of isolated facts and anecdotes, but a series of more or less coherent processes with beginnings, middles, and ends. Migrations, wars, or depressions are not whims of an unpredictable fate, but events which follow with various degrees of necessity from certain other events. Individual facts are intelligible only as parts of comprehensive wholes.

It goes without saying that with respect to their conception of facts the Marxist and the *Tractatus'* worldviews are incompatible. Wittgenstein's attitude toward the world is anti-ideological to an extreme. But Wittgenstein's conception of facts does not only undermine "holistic" theories like that of Marx, Hegel, Toynbee, or Jaspers, but common sense perceptions of reality as well. Common sense, after all, does perceive facts in terms of causal sequences. When Wittgenstein denounces the belief in causality as "superstition," he criticizes the modern everyday understanding of the world.[18] By eradicating this "superstition" from one's mind, by seeing things as they really are, one perceives facts in a highly unusual way. One sees them, as it were, in a frozen frame— essentially unconnected to what comes before and after. One sees them *"sub specie aeternitatis."*[19] And seeing them in this way, seeing them outside of their causal and temporal context, renders them inevitably mysterious—as mysterious as the objects of de Chirico's "metaphysical" paintings.[20] For facts thusly perceived lose the explainability which they have when they can be related to other facts. They turn into objects of a profoundly disinterested contemplation, a contemplation of philosophical minds who in no way partake in the concerns and views of everyday life.

A measure of how deeply Wittgenstein undercuts common sense is his devaluation of science. The prevailing view of the modern age is that science describes the world as it actually is—as opposed to religion, myth, or other nonscientific worldviews which indulge in unverifiable speculations, and which disguise, distort, or omit the facts as they are in themselves. But Wittgenstein suggests that the scientific description of the world represents only one kind of understanding besides several other ones. The scientific interpretation of the world, according to the *Tractatus,* is not a correction of mistaken views, but an alternative conception which is neither more nor less valid than any other conception. What scientists call "the laws of nature" do not "explain" the facts of nature, but simply incorporate them into a conceptual framework to which scientists happen to be committed:

The whole modern conception of the world is founded on the illusion that the so-called laws of nature are the explanations of natural phenomena.

Thus people today stop at the laws of nature, treating them as something inviolable, just as God and Fate were treated in past ages. And in fact both are right and both are wrong: Though the view of the ancients is clearer in so far as they have a clear and acknowledged

terminus, while the modern system tries to make it look as if
everything were explained.[21]

The ancients and science-minded contemporaries are both right in that
they are both at liberty to choose a conceptual framework into which
they can incorporate their data. But they are both wrong in assuming that
their descriptions represent the world as it actually is. Their conceptual
frameworks are nothing but constructs which may facilitate the
organization of facts by subsuming them to a unified method of
representation, and which may even answer to certain aesthetic or
emotional needs, but which turn into falsifying ideologies as soon as they
are taken to be the means to reveal the true view of the world.[22]

The actual state of the world is as little seen by the scientist as by the
faithful adherent to any religion or other *Weltanschauung.* Nor is it seen
any better by those who are involved in the ordinary business of life. The
true nature of the world is revealed alone to the philosopher who
carefully analyzes language, separating genuine statements from
obfuscating gibberish, and who conducts a parallel analysis of reality. By
doing so, he separates what there is from all the connections and
constructs which people may assume for one reason or another. As the
analytic philosopher is not taken in by empty verbiage, so he is also freed
of any ontological illusions. To this kind of philosopher, the world
appears as what it is: A conglomerate of facts, stripped of all connections,
values, and significance, and—paradoxically—"limited" by a transcendence which has no existence.

*

With respect to common sense worldviews or philosophical theories
of reality, the bare, disconnected facts are what is real, what constitutes
the world. But with respect to the total ontology of the *Tractatus,* the
facts are not quite yet what is real. One still needs to engage in further
analysis to arrive at the ultimate substance of the world. This further
analysis is, again, structured by the analysis of language.

The entirety of (meaningful) language divides into propositions, and
these divide further into elementary propositions. Elementary propositions, in turn, divide into "names," i.e., words which stand for objects in
the world. "Names" are the ultimate atoms of language.[23]

In analogy to this linguistic analysis, the entirety of reality divides into fact, and facts divide into states of affairs (or elementary facts, as one might say). States of affairs divide into "objects," the ultimate atoms of reality.[24]

Unfortunately, Wittgenstein never provided any examples of elementary propositions and "names," or of states of affairs and "objects." (The examples of the "elementary" propositions mentioned earlier in this chapter are only *relatively* elementary, introduced to illustrate the logical relation between them and more complex propositions. They would have to be analyzed much further to arrive at what Wittgenstein envisaged as elementary.)[25] It is, in fact, impossible to pinpoint anything as an "object" without running afoul of the conditions of simplicity which have to be met by something to qualify as an "object"[26]—which is one reason why Wittgenstein abandoned this idea of analysis in his later philosophy. At the time when he wrote the *Tractatus,* however, Wittgenstein was convinced that there *must* be "objects," for otherwise it seemed inexplicable how words, propositions, and language in general can have meaning. Thus he postulated a "substance" which, as it were, underlay all of reality:

Objects are simple.[27]

Objects make up the substance of the world. That is why they cannot be composite.[28]

Substance is what subsists independently of what is the case.[29]

Objects, the unalterable, and the subsistent are one and the same.[30]

Objects are what is unalterable and subsistent; their configuration is what is changing and unstable.[31]

Facts, according to the *Tractatus,* are complexes which are composed of the atomic elements called "objects." As these complexes are only one combination among several possible ones, they are "alterable" and "unstable." The only thing which remains the same, and thus is "stable," are the "objects themselves." They have the kind of firmness or solidity which the facts of the world lack.

Although a substance of the world is postulated primarily to explain the meaningfulness of language, one should not overlook the quasi-theological connotations which Wittgenstein's analysis of facts into an underlying substance carries.[32] That the facts of the world are not the rock bottom of an ultimate reality, that they are not as "hard" as Positivists think them to be, lends a certain insubstantiality to the world of facts. Facts are characterized by a transitoriness which in the Western tradition has often been ascribed to all "worldly" things. They are cursed, as it were, by the *vanitas mundi et fuga saeculi* which time and again has inspired thinkers to look and long for a realm where time does not hold sway, and where things exist without corruption or change. By conceiving of an unalterable substance, Wittgenstein has given himself a vanishing point in the direction of which the facts of the world can be transcended. This transcendence does not provide the metaphysical refuge which earlier faiths may have offered, but it does render the world as the disintegrating abode that both the theologians of the past and the writers of Modernism so often portray: a place of corruption which cannot provide a final home for the human spirit.

Hofmannsthal: "A Letter"

Hugo von Hofmannsthal was born in Vienna in 1874. He wrote very successful poetry between the age of seventeen and twenty-five. After a crisis (which is reflected in the letter discussed below) he turned to writing drama and criticism exclusively. One of his best known later works is his libretto for Richard Strauss' *Der Rosenkavalier*. He died in 1929.

"A Letter" (generally known as the "Chandos Letter") was written in 1902. It is the fictional response of Philipp Lord Chandos to his friend Francis Bacon, who had inquired why Lord Chandos, formerly a successful author, was not writing anymore. Although the letter is dated "August 22, 1603," the explanations offered by Lord Chandos are typical of the experience of twentieth century writers. "A Letter" describes a perception of the world which centers around the feeling that things are falling apart, and that there is no legitimate way anymore to pull them together.

Following are two key passages from the letter:

My case, in short, is this: I have completely lost the ability to think or talk about anything coherently.[33]

My mind compelled me to see everything, which was mentioned in such conversations, uncannily closely: As I had once seen a piece of my skin through a magnifying glass, which made it look like a vast field with furrows and hollows, thus I began to see people and their activities. I could not grasp them anymore with the simplifying view of habit. For me everything fell to pieces, and the pieces disintegrated into still smaller fragments, and nothing could be held together by a unifying concept.[34]

Lord Chandos' present predicament is contrasted with his past creative accomplishments, and an experience of life which integrated all aspects of reality into one comprehensive unity:

In those days I experienced a sort of intoxication in which everything seemed to be part of an all-embracing unity: The spiritual and the physical did not seem to be opposed to each other, nor were the court's culture and the animal kingdom, art and life, solitude and social life; . . .[35]

Lord Chandos' difficulties started with an increasing inability to discourse on a high level of abstraction, to formulate judgments which involved terms like "spirit," "soul," or "body." Such abstract terms "disintegrated in his mouth like rotten mushrooms."[36] The inability spread "like rust," until the very mundane statements of everyday life were affected. Lord Chandos finds himself unable to utter or understand such pronouncements as "Sheriff N. is a bad man," or "tenant M. is in an enviable position." The tacit and explicit understanding of the world which finds expression in ordinary communication disintegrates for him.

Once the evaluations, which social conventions place on things, are gone, the world of bare facts becomes chaotic. (If all facts are on the same level, there is no reason anymore to consider some as important, others as negligible, and so forth.) There is no predictable way in which Lord Chandos will react to this or that detail of reality. Those things which ordinarily are considered grandiose may leave him completely unmoved, and the most inconspicuous objects may rouse in him the most profound emotions.[37] Any plausible relation among the facts themselves, and the facts and the perceiving individual, has vanished.

To escape this chaotic world Lord Chandos tries to take refuge in the conceptual cosmos of the classical tradition (a move which in some ways parallels the desperate conversion of some modern artists and writers to the well-ordered world of Catholicism). He contemplates the

philosophical systems of Seneca and Cicero. But in the end he finds
himself unable to enter that world:

> These concepts—I understood them well. I saw the beautiful play of
> their relations—like dazzling fountains which keep the golden balls in
> motion. But these concepts related only to each other. The deepest
> and most personal of my own thoughts remained excluded from them.
> Among them I was seized by a most profound loneliness. I felt like
> someone who was confined to a park full of eyeless statues. I fled that
> park.[38]

Ultimately Lord Chandos is condemned to live in a world without
structure, and thus to be silent. He keeps up a minimum of external
activities, such as the administration of his estate, but it is clear that his
self is not identical with such external occupations. He does not live, but
plays a role. His real world and self have been dissolved by an inexorable
fate; the forces and conditions of the modern world.

Trakl: "In the Evening My Heart"

The laconic conjunction of factual statements is one of the most typical
techniques of modern poetry. In most contexts it expresses the
perceived disconnectedness of the facts, or a deep indifference of the
perceiver toward the world. It obviously corresponds to an experience of
reality which is also expressed in Wittgenstein's conception of facts.

The following poem by Georg Trakl[39] is an example of this world
experience:

IN THE EVENING MY HEART

In the evening one hears the screams of bats;
Two black horses jump about the field;
The rustling of red maple trees.
The wanderer sees the small pub at the side of the road.
Splendid the taste of nuts and young wine;
Splendid: to drunkenly stumble through darkening woods.
Painful bells chime through black boughs;
Dew is dripping on the face.

There are no rhymes, nor any other elements of traditional poetic form. The basic structure of the poem consists of added-together statements of fact. The statements are terse, in some cases reduced to telegram-style notes. They do not add up to a coherent description of a scene or an event; the facts singled out by the poet are not related to each other in any coherent way. On the contrary: they are carefully selected to create an environment of random disconnectedness. Although the arbitrariness of the conjunctions in Trakl's poem is not of the kind aimed at by Dadaists or Surrealists ("the encounter on an operating table of an umbrella and a sewing machine"), within the relatively realistic frame of the poem the emphasis is clearly on showing the fragmentation of reality.

In accordance with this fragmentation, the self, as much as it appears in the poem, is disjointed as well. In the fourth line it appears as "the wanderer," seen from the outside, a fact among other facts. The fifth line gives a short glance, as it were, of the inside of the wanderer, a sense impression which is not connected to anything else in the poem. The self is totally depersonalized in the last line, where the dew drips on "the" face. By avoiding "his" or "my" face, the body of the person is objectified to an extreme, is reduced to a lifeless object among objects. The emotion which occurs, by contrast, is projected into something inanimate, the sound of the bells. Thus, whatever personal details come up in the poem are scattered among the facts of the world as randomly as everything else. And the one human movement which is mentioned is, befittingly, a "stumbling," a movement which connotes uncertainty of direction, and a loss of power and deliberation. It represents, symbolically, the kind of action that is possible within a fragmented world. It corresponds to a state of affairs which is thoroughly devoid of meaning, goals, coherence, and orientation.

Ball: "Caravan"

One of the most characteristic tendencies in modern poetry (as in Modern Art generally) is the drift toward dissolution. On all levels of expression, in the domain of concepts as well as in those of external structures, poets effected or consciously intended the disintegration of comprehensive units into their various elements.

Dissolution was achieved in modern poetry in serious as well as in playful ways. T.S. Eliot's *The Waste Land* represents this dissolution in a highly intellectualized fashion. "Caravan" (composed by Hugo Ball in

1917), is, by contrast, a graphic and playful representation of the tendency toward entropy in Modern Art. Its sounds, carefully separated from any cognitive content, suggest the noises of a caravan on the move. The variety of the typefaces corresponds to the variety of men, animals, and goods typical of a caravan. But what is important with respect to the forms of modern poetry is the dissolution of the uniformity of typography which had become standard for printed poetry. By visually reducing the multiplicity of greatly varied contents to the unity of a single typeface, a certain tranquility was bestowed on even the most unusual poetic texts. This unity is exploded in Ball's poem. Typographically, no line is like any other. Visually, the elements of the text come apart. Their centrifugal tendency represents graphically what in essence occurs in all other areas of Modern Art.

In connection with Eliot's *The Waste Land* it has been pointed out that the unities of language, style, and ideology were dissolved into a conglomerate of languages, styles, and worldviews. Compared with Dante's *Comedia Divina,* where the dogma and the religious symbolism of medieval Christianity informs virtually every aspect of content and form, Eliot's *The Waste Land* is a collage of scattered bits and pieces of faiths and styles. (Eliot's numerous references in *The Waste Land* to Dante are, in part, to remind the reader of the lost unity.) And in connection with Ball's "Dirge" it was pointed out that among Futurists and Dadaists attempts were made to "liberate" words from the grammatical structures, such as sentences, to which they are usually subsumed. What, in spite of their obvious differences, is common to the early Eliot and the Dadaists is their dissolution into fragments of what traditionally has been treated as wholes.

Other prominent examples of fragmented unities can be found throughout the spectrum of modern poetry. The fact that Free Verse became the predominant form for modern poets is a case in point. Free Verse is a rebellion against the confining structures of such inherited forms as the sonnet, against rhyme schemes, and against counted meters. It is, in a limited and symbolic way, the assertion of anarchic tendencies against structures which are felt to be superimposed from without on a material which ought to express without restraints. As Free Verse is a rebellion against rhetorical and metrical superimpositions, so the experiments of Futurists and Dadaists are rebellions against the perceived superimpositions of grammar. This rebellion went in part so far as to "liberate" individual letters from the unit of the word, thus dissolving language to the point where the elements of language (letters) became

KARAWANE

jolifanto bambla ô falli bambla
grossiga m'pfa habla horem
égiga goramen
higo bloiko russula huju
hollaka hollala
anlogo bung
blago bung
blago bung
bosso fataka
ü üü ü
schampa wulla wussa ólobo
hej tatta gôrem
eschige zunbada
wulubu ssubudu uluw ssubudu
tumba ba- umf
kusagauma
ba - umf

Figure 3. Hugo Ball, *Caravan,* (1917)

elements in graphic and other pictorial designs. Not only Dadaists, but also Cubists and Surrealists treated isolated letters or syllables as quasi-objects, which appear in their pictures as things next to coffee cups and tobacco pipes.

Two further kinds of dissolution which have significantly influenced the shape of modern poetry are those of logic and realism. Freud had pointed out that the stream of consciousness which is formed by reason is different from that of Free Association. Freudian Psychoanalysis was to a great extent based on the idea of reading the Unconscious by deactivating ratiocination, i.e., by allowing the natural jumble of pictures, thoughts, memories, or hopes to emerge without imposing the ordering control of the conscious mind on them. Surrealist writers cultivated this technique in their "automatic writing." And in their theories, Surrealists put great stress on the idea that the order of reason was an oppressive and falsifying one, and that the revitalization of life is dependent on smashing its structure in a revolutionary upheaval. In conjunction with this idea, the Surrealists also advocated the seeming disorder of dreams against the restrictive order of reality, the kind of order which was accepted as the only valid one by realistic writers or painters. The idea was that by dissolving the structure of reality it was possible to destroy a false front. By destroying the ordinary order of things (by arranging for the "encounter on an operating table of an umbrella and a sewing machine") the Surrealists hoped to find an existence which was free of dogmatic assumptions and illusions, and thus free of the ills which, according to them, keep haunting the Western world. It is within this context that Ball's typographical rebellion has to be seen.

Keaton: *The General*

Joseph Francis "Buster" Keaton was born in 1895 in Piqua, Kansas. From his parents, who were vaudeville actors, he learned acrobatics and mime. In 1917 he made his first film, *The Butcher Boy*. During the twenties he directed and acted in numerous shorts and features. His career declined with the advent of sound movies, which put an end to the production of silent films and de-emphasized the art of mime. He experienced a modest come-back when connoisseurs rediscovered his outstanding talent in the forties. Keaton died in California in 1966.

The General was filmed in 1926. It is a comedy of disconnectedness. Its story is based on an actual episode from the Civil War: A Union spy, with

Figure 4. Scene from *The General,* (1926)

the help of half a dozen men, steals the locomotive "The General" from the Confederates, and flees North, destroying in the process as much of the Southern line as possible. Buster Keaton (without any philosophical intentions) transformed this story into a film in which the world appears as if it were constructed according to the ontology of Wittgenstein's *Tractatus.*

The disconnectedness begins with the film character of Buster Keaton itself: He is a man who displays the same intense, unsmiling facial expression in whatever situation he finds himself, whether he is attacking as an enemy soldier, proposing to his fiancee, or oiling the wheels of his locomotive. There is no correlation between his facial expression and the situation in which he finds himself, and thus seemingly no correspondence between his inner state and the external context. Whatever he is engaged in seems oddly out of touch with his state of mind. That is part of the comic appeal of his *persona.*

A good many scenes in *The General* seem to be hilarious illustrations of sections 6.373 and 6.374 of the *Tractatus:* "The world is independent of my will" . . . "Even if all that we wish for were to happen, still this would only be a favor granted by fate, so to speak . . ." For example, at the beginning of the film (and the Civil War) Keaton tries to enlist, and he tries harder than everybody else. But in the end, due to circumstances beyond his control, he is the only one not in uniform, and thus the object of the contempt of his fiancee and her family. Or when the Northern patrol steals his "General," he rushes to another locomotive which is ready to pull a flatbed full of troops into action. He starts the engine and follows the thieves in hot pursuit. But the troop transport is not hitched to the engine, and thus stays behind.

In this way, much of the film's sequence of events is made up of episodes which illustrate the incongruity of will and action. In a situation where time is of the essence, Keaton stops the locomotive to quickly replenish his firewood supply. In his hurry he does not watch where he throws the logs, and thus does not notice that not only do they fall on the other side of the tender, but even knock off logs which are already on it. And in the Battle of Marietta he draws his sword to point out the firing line to the cannoneers. The blade, however, flies off the handle and lands, by sheer coincidence, in the back of a sniper who had been picking off his comrades. During the same battle, he finally tries to fire the cannon himself. Inexplicably, the barrel moves upward, and the shot goes straight into the air.   Keaton's effort seems to be wasted. By coincidence, however, the shell destroys a dam, causing a sudden flood. The enemy soldiers, who are in the middle of fording the river, are washed away, thus saving the Southerners from a surprise attack.

Many of these scenes are not simply instances of intentions not being realized. On several occasions things turn out the way they are supposed to—but for reasons totally unrelated to the intentions of the actors. The episodes of the drawn sword and the misfired cannon shot are illustrations of this kind of case. For the sniper *is* to be incapacitated, and the enemy soldiers *are* to be prevented from crossing the river. But these tasks are accomplished in a way no one had planned.

One of the most famous episodes of the movie is Keaton's struggle with the mortar which is hitched to his locomotive. It can be seen as a drawn out illustration of Wittgenstein's view that everything is "accidental." After Keaton has loaded the gun and ignited the fuse to fire a volley at the enemy ahead of him, the barrel suddenly goes down and is now aimed at his own vehicle. All his attempts to avert the disaster turn out to be futile. Just when the shot goes off, his locomotive turns into a curve and is out of danger. At the same time, the enemy engine has completed the curve and is directly in the line of fire. The booming explosion which almost derails their locomotive creates in the Northern party the (totally mistaken) conviction that Keaton's train constitutes a dangerously superior force.

The way *The General* represents reality can be described as a joyful subversion of the ordinary connections which hold the facts of the world together. In this film there is no predictable nexus between one event and another: anything can result from anything else. Thus Keaton gathers military intelligence, because he is *hiding* from the enemy. Or he sets out to rescue his "General," but in the process rescues his fiancee. He is finally honored and promoted—not for his real valor and exploits, but because coincidentally he stumbles over a Northern commander who had passed out, and whom he can thus take prisoner. Nowhere in this film is there a plausible connection between an action and its results.

Another way in which *The General* expounds the theme of disconnectedness is by showing displaced behavior. As Keaton's facial expression is only coincidentally in accord with an external situation, so the behavior of the protagonists is often entirely unrelated to the situation in which it is found. When Keaton calls on his fiancee, he stands in front of the door in the expectation that it will be opened by her—after he is done with slickening his hair, brushing his jacket, etc. But all the while his fiancee is already standing behind him on the porch, observing his discreet preparations. Or when he runs after his locomotive with a group of outraged travelers, making menacing gestures towards the thieves, he doesn't notice that after a while he is all alone, the other travelers having become discouraged by the hopeless pursuit and fallen behind. Under the circumstances, his menacing behavior is ludicrous.

The disconnectedness of the world of *The General* is symbolized by the incongruous role of uniforms in the film. When the locomotive thieves reach Northern territory, Union soldiers shoot at their leader because he is still wearing a Southern uniform. And when Keaton, upon his successful return from the North, waves enthusiastically at the first men in grey, they shoot at him because he is still clad in blue. Such happenings underscore once more that in this film there is no correspondence between inner and outer states, as little as between any other facts. In *The General's* world, the man in blue may or may not be a Northerner, and the man in grey may be friend as much as foe. Since in that world all connections are essentially "accidental," it is ultimately impossible to tell.

Due to the prominence of the railroad in *The General,* the hitching and unhitching of cars is a highly visible *leitmotif* in the entire film. This motif was certainly not chosen by Keaton for philosophical reasons. But considering the basic structure of disconnectedness in the film it is a fortunate coincidence that the precarious nature of the hitchings symbolizes elegantly the precarious nexus between the facts of this world.

Chandler: *The Long Goodbye*

Raymond Chandler was born in Chicago in 1888. From age nine on he was raised by his divorced mother in England. He received a classical education at Dulwich College in London, and until the outbreak of World War I he worked as a journalist. He served in the Canadian Army, and in 1919 he settled in Los Angeles. Until 1929 he worked, consecutively, as a journalist, an accountant, and an oil company executive. After the Stock Market crash of 1929 he started writing mystery fiction. *Black Mask* (a detective story magazine which Wittgenstein may well have read frequently[40]) published his first story in 1933. From then on he wrote regularly and successfully for the "pulps." In 1939 he published his first novel, *The Big Sleep. Farewell My Lovely* followed in 1940, *The High Window* in 1942, *The Lady in the Lake* in 1943, *The Little Sister* in 1949, *The Long Goodbye* in 1954, and *Playback* in 1958. He authored and co-authored the movie scripts for *Double Indemnity, The Blue Dahlia,* and *The Unseen.* The features of his writing which became best known

are his realism (which earned him the label "hard-boiled"), his mastery
of American slang, and his unusually colorful metaphors. Chandler died in
La Jolla in 1959.

Modern literary fiction is characterized by a high degree of
disintegration of those features which traditionally served as a means of
unification in works of art: time, place, character, and plot. It is typical for
modern narrative fiction that time-sequences are broken up into
discontinuous pieces, that locations are deliberately jumbled or
ambiguous, that the slowly developed and well-rounded characters of
nineteenth century novels are replaced by character-fragments or
disembodied streams of consciousness, and that plots are either absurd
or nonexistent. Such authors as Proust, Joyce, Kafka, Dos Passos, or
Beckett created the paradigms of modern fiction. Their prose created the
same fragmented and chaotic view of the world which is conveyed by
such modern poets as Eliot or Trakl, the collages of Dadaists, or the
Theatre of the Absurd.

The detective or mystery story, a *genre* which could not have come
about before the ascent of the modern world, is seemingly thoroughly
traditional in form, and for this reason has largely been ignored in
discussions of serious modern fiction. But an argument can be made to
the effect that mysteries, by their peculiar form, convey the same basic
image of reality as other modern works of art, and that for that reason
they are as legitimate an expression of twentieth century consciousness
as the works which are accepted as truly representative of the spirit of
this age.[41] The reason why mysteries can be considered as representative
of the experience which perceives reality as disintegrating is the very fact
that they so faithfully cling to the unity of character and plot. For the
construction of a narrative by means of an easily identifiable protagonist
(exemplified by such schematic and poster-like figures as Chandler's
detective Philip Marlowe) and a plot which is calculated according to the
requirements of puzzle cases and the mechanics of suspense is so
obviously artificial, that the underlying anarchy and incoherence of the
depicted world becomes all the more apparent. The mystery story
presupposes a world with an infinite number of possibilities, a world
which is labyrinthean in its complexity, an environment in which an
unforseeable number of things can happen at any time. In this world, the
piecemeal investigations and encounters of the individual detective
establish, for the duration of the story, connections which create some
sort of ephemeral order. But the lack of substantiality of this order is
plain. What the investigations of the "private eye" reveal is not a cosmic

order, but a private world. The real character of the world in which the detective operates is disconnectedness and chaos. The environment of the mystery story is essentially modern and urban. It presupposes the anonymity of mass societies, the multiplicity of cultures and subcultures in sprawling metropolitan landscapes, the diversity of social roles which individuals can play, the innumerable locations within relatively easy reach of each other, in which people can live or hide, the vast possibilities in which crimes can be committed, the intricate law enforcement agencies with their extensive files, laboratories, specialists, and organizations, and the complexity of social relations in which isolated individuals are free or obliged to look out for their personal interests. Detective work would be limited or impossible in a pre-industrial society of small communities, where everyone's life was in more or less plain view of everyone else. Stories of hidden identities, as that of Dr. Jekyll and Mr. Hyde, are logically tied to the big city. Only in big cities, or enclaves of complex societies, have facts become so mysterious that their connection requires special investigations.

The Los Angeles of Chandler's private investigator Philip Marlowe is just such an urban landscape. In *The Long Goodbye* Marlowe muses:

> Far off the banshee wail of police sirens rose and fell, never for very long completely silent. Twenty-four hours a day somebody is running, somebody else is trying to catch him. Out there in the night of a thousand crimes people were dying, being maimed, cut by flying glass, crushed against steering wheels or under heavy tires. People were being beaten, robbed, strangled, raped, and murdered. People were hungry, sick, bored, desperate with loneliness or remorse or fear, angry, cruel, feverish, shaken by sobs. A city no worse than others, a city rich and vigorous and full of pride, a city lost and beaten and full of emptiness. It all depends on where you sit, and what your own private score is. I didn't have one. I didn't care.[42]

Because of the unfathomable diversity of the city, and the unpredictability of events, the individual is left with a pervasive feeling of insecurity and darkness concerning one's fate:

> 'Man never knows what he's up against in this town'
>   A prowl car cop brought in a drunk with a bloody ear. We went towards the elevator. 'You're in trouble, boy,' Spranklin told me in the elevator. 'Heap of trouble'. It seemed to give him a vague satisfaction. 'A

guy can get hisself in a lot of trouble in this town.'
The elevator man turned his head and winked at me. I grinned.
'Don't try nothin', boy.' Spranklin told me severely. 'I shot a man
once. Tried to break. They ate my ass off.'
'You get it coming and going, don't you?'
He thought it over. 'Yeah,' he said, 'Either way they eat your ass off.
It's a tough town.'[43]

A special case of the disconnectedness and unpredictability of facts is
the dissociation of the individual from his or her social environment. The
social isolation of Marlowe runs like a *leitmotif* through all of Chandler's
novels. In *The Long Goodbye* Marlowe gives the following description of
himself:

> I am a lone wolf, unmarried, getting middle-aged, and not rich. I've
> been in jail more than once and I don't do divorce business. I like
> liquor and women and chess and a few other things. The cops don't
> like me too well, but I know a couple I get along with. I'm a native son,
> born in Santa Rosa, both parents dead, no brothers or sisters, and when
> I get knocked off in a dark alley sometime, if it happens, as it could to
> anyone in my business, and to plenty of people in any business or no
> business at all these days, nobody will feel that the bottom has dropped
> out of his or her life.[44]

The lone wolf existence of Marlowe is not an abnormal fate in
Chandler's world. Marlowe's investigations usually bring to light that
those relations which seem close, intact, and normal are in reality empty,
desperate, fake, or based on one-sided or mutual exploitation. People
relate to each other as if they were things. The alienation which
characterizes their relations to the world at large pervades their most
intimate commitments. For this reason, Chandler time and again
elaborates the theme of looking at a person as an inanimate object, or as a
creature which is treated as such an object. In *The Long Goodbye*
Marlowe says: "He looked at me like an entomologist looking at a beetle;"
"He looked at me as if I was a cigarette stub, or an empty chair." In *The
Big Sleep* one finds: "He looked at me as if I were a photograph;" "He
looked me over without haste, without interest, as if he was looking at a
slab of cold meat;" and so forth.
    In this world of disconnected objects and persons, personal identity
becomes a matter of deep concern, almost an obsession. If it is impossible

to find a hold in the world of objects or by means of genuine personal relations, the self becomes the only reliable center of one's existence. In a world which is in disarray and decaying in every respect, Marlowe defines his own existence and conduct with incorruptible rigidity, sparing neither his own or other people's feelings. He is what Chandler argued a detective in a modern mystery ought to be. This ideal is described by Chandler in his essay "The Simple Art of Murder" (written in 1950) as follows:

> But down these mean streets a man must go who is not himself mean, who is neither tarnished nor afraid. The detective in this kind of story must be such a man. He is the hero; he is everything . . . He must be, to use a rather weathered phrase, a man of honor . . . He must be the best man in his world . . . He will take no man's money dishonestly and no man's insolence without a due and dispassionate revenge. He is a lonely man and his pride is that you will treat him as a proud man or be very sorry you ever saw him.[45]

Marlowe is the exact opposite of Terry Lennox, the man with whom Marlowe is preoccupied throughout *The Long Goodbye*. Lennox is a drifter. He changes his name and his appearance as circumstances require. He is a man "who has learned how to roll with a punch." He allows himself to play the husband of a rich woman who needs a front for her amorous adventures, and he does not mind being a "kept poodle." Marlowe tells him:

> You were a nice guy because you had a nice nature. But you were just as happy with mugs or hoodlums as with honest men. Provided the hoodlums spoke fairly good English and had fairly acceptable table manners.[46]

Lennox is not a criminal, and he is pleasant company. Marlowe likes him and goes out of his way to help him. But in the end he says goodbye to him—for no other reason than the fact that (without malice, and only due to unusual circumstances) Lennox had impersonated a man, that he had played the role of someone who he was not. The wrong which Lennox committed was to sacrifice his identity, to fall apart like the rest of the world, to vanish in the maelstrom of disconnected facts.

For all of Chandler's realism, it is clear that the figure of Philip Marlowe is unreal. His honesty is too extreme, his overcoming of temptations too schematic, his adherence to principles too unfeeling. He is not an outstanding character in the world in which he lives and operates, but a figure that is constructed as a contrast *to* this world. He is not meant to show that there are good people as well as bad people, but serves more as a measure by which one can gauge how much the personalities, morals, institutions, and the social fabric in general have already disintegrated. Marlowe does not stem the movement toward entropy, but rather makes it visible.

One of the literary devices that Chandler used repeatedly is the dispassionate enumeration of unrelated facts. Passages like the following from *The Long Goodbye* occur at intervals throughout his novels:

> A tethered horse dozed wearily under a clump of live oaks. A brown Mexican sat on the ground and ate something out of a newspaper. A tumbleweed rolled lazily across the road and came to rest against a piece of granite outcrop, and a lizard that had been there an instant before disappeared without seeming to move at all.[47]

Such recounting of facts is reminiscent of enumerations in the poetry of Trakl and other modern writers, and it is in accord with the p.q, etc., structure of reality which Wittgenstein ascribes to the world. Its repeated occurrence accentuates the worldview which underlies all the ephemeral connections which Marlowe is able to make on his journey through the labyrinth of modern Los Angeles.

The most striking way, however, in which Chandler suggests or reminds the reader of the disconnectedness and chaotic conjunction of all facts are the distinct metaphors with which his stories are virtually littered. In these metaphors, the basic disparity of all facts is symbolically represented by the disparity of the things compared. The following are examples from *The Long Goodbye:*

> (The cigarette) tasted like a high fog strained through cotton wool.

> His surprise was as thin as the gold on a weekend wedding ring.

> He was about as hard to see as the Dalai Lama.

> I was walking the floor and listening to Khachaturyan working in a tractor factory. He called it a violin concerto. I called it a loose fan belt . . .

I belonged to Idle Valley like a pearl onion on a banana split.

. . . and remember that a Crane [Dectective Agency] operator is to a cheap shamus like you what Toscanini is to an organ grinder's monkey.

He has as much charm as a steel puddler's underpants.

An hour crawled by like a sick cockroach.

And the commercials would have sickened a goat raised on barbed wire and broken beer bottles.[48]

What makes Chandler's metaphors so distinctive is the great distance which lies between the thing or action which is to be characterized, and the object to which it is compared. Without there being *some* kind of remote similarity between the compared items, the metaphors would, of course, not be as witty as they are. But the dissimilarity between the compared items is so great that in most cases the comparison borders on the absurd, and it is this feature of Chandler's metaphors which makes them significant. For underneath all the constructions of character, plot and metaphors, Chandler's world is out of joint and absurd. Its scattered facts, if they are to make any sense, have to be pulled together by artifice and brute artistic force. And no amount of unity effected by the combinations of the private eye can hide the vast disunity of the wasteland which lies beyond the story's artificial construction.

Picasso: "Still Life: Newspaper, Wineglass And Pipe"

Pablo Ruiz Picasso was born in 1881 in Malaga, Spain. He moved to Paris in 1900, where he was to live during most of his highly productive years (eventually becoming a French citizen). During his career as painter, sculptor, ceramicist, and engraver, he developed many styles. His most notable accomplishment as a trend-setter of Modern Art, however, was his creation of Cubism, a style which he then developed in close collaboration with George Braque during the seven years prior to World War I, and which was to exert the most profound influence on modern artists everywhere. World fame came with with his painting "Guernica" (1936), in which he employed modern forms to create a shocking

Figure 5. Pablo Picasso, *Still Life: Newspaper, Wineglass and Pipe,* (1914)

memorial to a Spanish town bombed by German planes during the Spanish Civil War. For the rest of his life Picasso was considered an exemplar of the modern artist, and his works the epitome of Modern Art. He died in Moegins, France, in 1973.

Picasso's "Demoiselles d'Avignon" (1907) is usually considered the first Cubist painting. The most outstanding feature of the Cubist technique is the dissolution of objects into an abstract composition of lines, surfaces, and colors. The initial objects—typically inconspicuous items such as bottles, glasses, pipes, newspapers, or musical instruments —are still recognizable, but their visual aspects are playfully varied in forms which serve no presentational function. Each picture represents, as it were, the process of the aesthetic dissolution of objects. To further emphasize the disintegrative tendencies of the materials of their compositions, the Cubists even began to paste such nonpainterly materials as newspaper clippings, labels, or wallpaper scraps on their canvases, thus foreshadowing such work as Kurt Schwitter's Dada collages.

"Still Life: Newspaper, Wineglass And Pipe" (1914) is a gouache and pencil sketch. Still lives have always been compositions in which objects have been assembled somewhat arbitrarily, thus emphasizing the nonpragmatic context in which things are to be seen in aesthetic contemplation. In spite of the apparent realism of traditional still lives, what is important is not the depiction of objects on a canvas, but the mode of their representation. And outstanding old masters of the *genre,* such as Willem Kalf, painted objects like lemon peels with extraordinary close attention to the nuances of color and surface, foreshadowing the nonrepresentational paintings which were to be cultivated in the twentieth century. The apparent materialism of seventeenth century Dutch still life paintings, in other words, is actually already a dissolution of material objects into aesthetic compositions.

The still life by Picasso (as most other still lives by Cubists) presents a "spiritualization" of matter as do those of the traditional still life masters, but its artistic intentions are more openly and directly expressed. Such items as the newspaper, the glass, and the table top are literally taken apart and transformed into abstract variations of lines and surfaces. The outlines of the table top and the paper, for example, are repeated in the way musical themes are repeated in compositions, and the dot matrix of the newsprint reappears several times as a visual echo of the original object. The realistic, three-dimensional objects with which the artist started are transformed into two-dimensional combinations of lines and surfaces.

In addition, the spatial relationships between various objects are transformed by the Cubist technique. The difference between foreground and background, does not exist, for example. The table space in the right half of the picture can be seen as both closer or further removed from the viewer than the newspaper, and the detailed items on that part of the table are suggestive of, but by no means identifiable as, pieces of paper stacked on top of each other. The glass is represented from several angles at once (thus introducing the "fourth dimension" of time into the composition), and the surface structure of table and paper do not end with the borders of these objects.

"Still Life: Newspaper, Wineglass And Pipe," and pictures like it, are neither realistic nor abstract (in the sense that Kandinsky's non-representational compositions are abstract). Rather, they demonstrate the process of abstraction, of transforming reality into a combination of visual elements. They represent an artistic deconstruction of the world. The purpose of this deconstruction is in part a radicalization of the artistic process as such, the manifestation of artistic autonomy with respect to the world, a world which is reduced to the building materials of artistic creation. The abridgment of the word "JOURNAL" to "JOU" provides a significant hint: The three letters are reminiscent of the French *"jouer,"* (to play), as much as they are of "journal," and the idea of dissolving the facts of reality into a game, or free play of forces, has always been a guiding concept in Western theories of art.[49] Cubist deconstruction, however, is also something like an ontological statement: It expresses that reality as such has no significance anymore, that it is senseless or futile to come to terms with it. While earlier art movements can be seen as attempting various ways to make *Reality* visible, to use art as a means to explore important aspects of the world, Cubism represents a determined withdrawal from, and overcoming of, the world. In this sense, Cubist compositions like "Still Life: Newspaper, Wineglass And Pipe" are documents of the overall tendency of Modern Art to exist apart from the world, to create its own aesthetic realm, and to admit fragments of reality only to the extent that they function as dematerialized, ahistorical pieces in an autonomously aesthetic context.

NOTES ON CHAPTER THREE

1. Wittgenstein, *Tractatus,* 5.

2. Wittgenstein's use of the "truth-tables" permits the mechanical determination of the truth or falsity of complex propositions. (Cf. *Tractatus* 4.31f and 5.1f.)

3. In section 5.1311 of the *Tractatus* Wittgenstein refers to an even more radical device of substitution, the so-called Sheffer Stroke. The logician Sheffer had shown that one can replace all four of the seemingly basic connectives by just one, namely the stroke /. "/" is defined in the following way: p/q = df. at least one of the two, p or q, is false. Based on this definition, one can write p.q as (p/q) / (p/q), or p⊃q as p/(q/q), and so forth. This substitution makes it strikingly clear that only the propositions themselves depict the facts of the world, while the connectives are nothing but devices with which to manipulate propositions on the level of language.

4. Wittgenstein, *Tractatus,* 4.0312.

5. *Ibid.,* 4.0621.

6. *Ibid.,* 5.44.

7. Emphases in the original.

8. *Ibid.,* 1.2.

9. *Ibid.,* 1.21.

10. *Ibid.,* 2.061.

11. *Ibid.,* 2.062.

12. *Ibid.,* 5.135.

13. Emphases in the original.

14. *Ibid.,* 6.37.

15. *Ibid.,* 6.3.

16. *Ibid.,* 6.373.

17. *Ibid.,* 6.374.

18. This is one of the reasons why Bertrand Russell's adoption of Wittgenstein's early thought is in part quite foreign to the outlook of the *Tractatus.* In the Introduction to his *The Philosophy of Logical Atomism,* which appeared in 1918, and which was profoundly influenced by Wittgenstein's early ideas, Russell writes:

> I shall set forth . . . a certain kind of logical doctrine, and on the basis of this a certain kind of metaphysic. The logic which I will advocate is atomistic, as opposed to the monistic logic of the people who more or less follow Hegel. When I say that my logic is atomistic,

I mean that I share the common sense belief that there are many separate things; I do not regard the apparent multiplicity of the world as consisting merely in phases and unreal divisions of a single indivisible Reality. (Bertrand Russell, "The Philosophy of Logical Atomism; Lectures Delivered in London in 1918." *Monist,* 28 (October 1918), 7.

Russell makes it look as if Logical Atomism were a defense of common sense against the arbitrary constructions of holistic philosophies like that of Hegel. He overlooks that Logical Atomism, particularly in Wittgenstein's version, is itself a philosophical construction which goes far beyond any ordinary conception of reality.

19. Wittgenstein, *Notebooks 1914-1916,* 7.10; 1916.

20. Cf. Chapter I, where seeing the world *"sub specie aeternitatis"* and de Chirico's "metaphysical" paintings are discussed. De Chirico's experience of seeing things out of context is particularly relevant here.

21. Wittgenstein, *Tractatus,* 6.371-6.372.

22. That the description of the world in terms of causes and effects, which is central to the scientific worldview, is only one way of describing reality, is also expressed in Wittgenstein's comment on the "law of causality": "The law of causality is not a law, but the form of a law" (*Tractatus,* 6.32). This "law" says that nothing in the world happens without a cause. But actual laws would be more specific, linking certain events with certain other events. The rule that every event is causally related to others is nothing but a directive to look at facts in a certain way. It is a stipulation of what scientific laws should be like.

23. Wittgenstein, *Tractatus,* 3.202.

24. Wittgenstein, *Tractatus,* 2; 2.01; 2.0272; 2.04.

25. The notion of absolute simplicity is discussed in detail in Wittgenstein's *Philosophical Investigations,* sections 46 ff., where the author criticizes his ideas of the *Tractatus* period.

26. Cf. Wittgenstein, *Tractatus,* 2.0201. This notion is criticized in the *Philosophical Investigations*, section 60.

27. Wittgenstein, *Tractatus,* 2.022.

28. *Ibid.,* 2.021.

29. *Ibid.,* 2.024.

30. *Ibid.,* 2.0227.

31. *Ibid.,* 2.0271.

32. Cf. Moran, *Toward the World and Wisdom of Wittgenstein's 'Tractatus',* 117.

33. Hugo von Hofmannsthal, *"Ein Brief,"* in *Ausgewählte Werke in Zwei Bänden,* vol. 2(Frankfurt: Büchergilde Gutenberg, 1961), 341, (my translation).

34. *Ibid.,* 342.

35. *Ibid.,* 340.

36. *Ibid.,* 341-42.

37. *Ibid.,* 345,347.

38. *Ibid.,* 343.

39. Cf. Chapter 1 and Trakl, "Zu Abend mein Herz," in *Die Dichtungen,* 75, (my translation).

40. Cf. Malcolm, *Ludwig Wittgenstein. A Memoir,* 35-36.

41. It is assumed here, of course, that not everything written in the twentieth century is representative of the age. Novels written in the style of *Anna Karenina,* e.g., are oddly out of place in the modern world, but do, in fact, still constitute the mass of contemporary fiction.

42. Raymond Chandler, *The Long Goodbye* (New York: Ballantine Books, 1971), 224.

43. *Ibid.,* 47.

44. *Ibid.,* 74.

45. Raymond Chandler, *The Simple Art of Murder* (New York: Ballantine Books, 1972), 20.

46. Chandler, *The Long Goodbye,* 310.

47. *Ibid.,* 197-98.

48. *Ibid.,* 43,63,65,69,80,92,93,111,81.

49. Cf. Friedrich Schiller, *The Aesthetic Education of Man,* and Hermann Hesse, *Magister Ludi.*

CHAPTER FOUR

THE VANISHING SELF

THE VANISHING SELF

"There are two godheads: the world and
my independent self."
—L. Wittgenstein: *Notebooks, 1914-1916*

It is common to define the self in relation to the world: the self is that
which is not the world, and the world is that which is not the self. The
self is distinguished from, and is in a certain sense opposed to, the world.

It is also common to conceive of the self as a person, i.e., as a being
with body, soul, and mind. Body, soul, and mind are part of the self, while
a person's possessions, e.g., are not part of the self, but part of the world.

Philosophers, however, have developed alternative definitions of the
self. While maintaining the idea that the world starts where the self ends,
various philosophers have developed different ideas as to where the
borderline between self and world ought to be drawn. Thus, while
ordinarily the body is considered part of the self, many philosophers
maintain that strictly speaking the body is part of the world rather than
the self. The body, according to these philosophers, is as external to the
real self as, e.g., a person's house. The body is something foreign and
manipulable, while the inner self is the real person who only temporarily
inhabits a physical abode.

Plato was the first Western philosopher who in this way drove a wedge
between the self and the body, and his view has had the most profound
effect on all later thinkers. The dualism of mind and body, in terms of
which philosophers and theologians came to think about the self, has
become a widely accepted commonplace in Western thought. It also
served as the guiding model for the speculations of the German Idealists,
the philosophers who (via Schopenhauer) influenced Wittgenstein's
early philosophy most directly.

These Idealists followed their predecessors in defining the self by
drawing a line between the self and the world, but they moved this
boundary even further into the interior of the person than Plato had
done. In distinguishing the true self from its external disguises, they
divested it not only of the body, but also of that part of the mind which
we call the "psyche"—the psyche being all such faculties as sensing,

imagining, feeling, intuiting, etc. The psyche, which increasingly became the subject matter of scientific investigations, and thus the object of external manipulations by drugs, mechanical stimuli, and so forth, was considered by these thinkers as an external condition of the self, just as the body, and not a genuine part of the innermost self itself. The psyche became part of the world.

The self proper, which the Idealists tried to define, was conceived as that which perceives the world. The world by definition is that which is perceived, while the act of perceiving is the innermost self, the "subject." The innermost self, then, is not an entity anymore, but an activity. It is not identical with any of the things which can be perceived and empirically investigated, but an act of the intellect.

Although Wittgenstein was not an Idealist when he wrote the *Tractatus* he was clearly influenced by this tradition of self-definition:

> The philosophical self is not the human being, not the human body, or the human psyche, with which psychology deals, but rather the metaphysical subject, the limit of the world—not a part of it.[1]

In his *Notebooks,* from which this *Tractatus* passage originated, Wittgenstein wrote further:

> The human body, however, my body in particular, is a part of the world among others, among animals, plants, stones, etc., etc.
> Whoever realizes this will not want to procure a pre-eminent place for his own body or for the human body.
> He will regard humans and animals quite naively as object which are similar and which belong together.[2]

> A stone, the body of a beast, the body of a man, my body, all stand on the same level.[3]

There is, in other words, a radical distinction between the real self, the "metaphysical subject," on the one hand, and the empirical, physical self on the other. And while the physical self belongs in the same class as the plants, beasts, and stones of the world, the real self stands outside of it.

The notion of the self as a "limit" occurs in the writings of Schopenhauer. In Schopenhauer's main work, *The World as Will and*

Representation, the author characterizes the relation between "subject" and "object" (self and world) as follows: "That which knows all things and is known by none is the subject . . . They [subject and object] limit each other immediately; where the object begins, the subject ceases."⁴ Self and world limit each other in somewhat the same way in which an island and the ocean limit each other: the ocean is the limit of the island, and the island the limit of the ocean. In this sense, the self is a limit of the world, and not part of it. (The island analogy is misleading, however, in that both ocean and island are separate, identifiable entities, while the "self" is not an entity existing independently of the world.)

The idea that the self as "metaphysical subject" is not part of the world is repeatedly expressed in Wittgenstein's early writings:

The subject does not belong to the world: rather, it is a limit of the world.⁵

Where *in* the world is a metaphysical subject to be found? You will say that this is exactly like the case of the eye and the visual field. But really you do *not* see the eye. And nothing *in the visual field* allows you to infer that it is seen by an eye.⁶

It would not be implausible to argue that for all practical purposes the metaphysical subject can be ignored, since there are the body and the psyche which are part of the world, and which together can be regarded as the practically relevant self. It is, after all, the empirical person that acts, has relationships with other people, transforms the world, etc. The "philosophical self," so the argument may go, is nothing but a theoretical construction which cannot shed much light on such concrete problems as the social and historical conditions of the twentieth century. Wittgenstein felt, however, that the metaphysical subject is more than a mere theoretical construct. The extra-mundane status of the metaphysical subject as conceived by Wittgenstein constitutes an understanding of the self which has practical implications at the most worldly levels of existence. For the "philosophical" self is, in Wittgenstein's eyes, the true self, and the large distance which separates this self from the world expresses a degree of estrangement which, according to the thinking of the *Tractatus,* is part of the human condition.

The distinction between the "philosophical" self and the world parallels the disconnectedness of will and the object of the will which was mentioned earlier.[7] Both the radical unworldliness of the "philosophical" self and the inefficacy of the will testify to a view in which the individual is a powerless plaything of fate, a mere object at the mercy of an alien world:

> The world is *given* me, i.e., my will confronts the world completely from outside, as something which is already complete . . .
>
> That is why we have the feeling of being dependent on an alien will.
> However this may be, we are in any event in a certain sense dependent, and what we are dependent on we can call God.
> In this sense, God would simply be fate, or, what is the same thing: The world—which is independent of our will.[8]

The practical implications of this attitude become explicit in the rules of conduct which Wittgenstein contemplates in his *Notebooks:*

> The only life that is happy is the life that can renounce the amenities of the world.
> To it the amenities are only so many graces of fate.[9]

> And yet in a certain sense it seems that not wanting is the only good.[10]

It would seem that the way of life which corresponds to this stoic ethic is essentially one of thought and study rather than of activism. Self-expression or self-realization does not come from anything that one "does" or "accomplishes," but through a purely contemplative life, a "life of knowledge":

> How can a man be happy at all, since he cannot ward off the misery of this world?
> Through the life of knowledge.
> The good conscience is the happiness which is granted by the life of knowledge.
> The life of knowledge is the life that is happy in spite of the misery of the world.[11]

Activities such as trying to make the world a better place to live in are particularly vain, according to this thinking. Neither the happiness nor the good conscience of the self are in any way related to the actual state of the world:

> *How* things are in the world is a matter of complete indifference for what is higher. God does not reveal himself *in* the world.[12]

> For it must be all one, as far as concerns the existence of ethics, whether there is living matter in the world or not. And it is clear that a world in which there is only dead matter is in itself neither good nor evil. Hence the world of living things can in itself be neither good nor evil.[13]

It will help to examine Wittgenstein's conception of the self by comparing it with that of the tradition from which it emerged. When Plato contrasted the true or inner self to the body and the external world, he also conceived of the supremacy of the inner self over the outer, of the rule of the mind over the material world. The inner self was characterized not only by superior insight, but also by a will to power. The ideal self should not blend passively into a given environment, but should impose its own designs on the world of the senses. The self was to be the active shaper of things, and the world the passive raw material for its creations. This emphasis on activity and power has characterized Western thinking ever since. It was one of the ideas that led to the domination of the West over the rest of the planet.

This relation between the self and the world is well stated in the following passage from Descartes' *Discourse on Method:*

> So it is that these old cities which, originally only villages, have become, through the passage of time, great towns, are usually so badly proportioned in comparison with those orderly towns which an engineer designs at will on some plane that, although the buildings, taken separately, often display as much art as those of the planned towns, or even more, nevertheless, seeing how they are placed, with a big one here, a small one there, and how they cause the streets to be bent and to be at different levels, one has the impression that they are more the product of chance than that of a human will operating according to reason.[14]

The self (the "human will") asserts itself by imposing its order on the chaotic raw material provided by history and nature. A prominent expression of this ideal are the carefully calculated and totally controlled environments exemplified by the geometrical patterns of the French gardens and castles of the Baroque period, by which Descartes was obviously inspired. This kind of architecture embodies a conception of the self in which effective power over the external world is supreme.

While in the time of Descartes the superior position of the rational will vis-a-vis nature was to a large extent expressed in aesthetics alone (in the French landscape architecture of the period, for example), the rule of the rational self envisaged by the Enlightenment of the eighteenth century was pragmatic, and significantly influenced by the scientific-technological thinking of the beginning Industrial Revolution. The human will was now in a position to effect the most profound changes in the world, to replace, in fact, the natural environment by a largely man-made world. Humanity seemed to have reached a position where nothing needed to be left to chance or fate, where rational selves would be in control of all major aspects of life. As Fichte put it in 1794: "To subject everything that is not rational, to rule it freely and according to his own laws—that is the ultimate purpose of man."[15]

It is hard to find a greater contrast than that between Fichte's aggressive self-assertion in the world, and Wittgenstein's total withdrawal from reality: "I can only make myself independent of the world—and so in a certain sense master it—by renouncing any influence on events."[16] Wittgenstein still mentions "mastering" the world, but what he means is an evasion of the mastery of the world over the self by reducing the self to a "point without extension."[17] By leaving body and psyche to the unpredictable fate of the world and retreating as an immaterialized "philosophical self," Wittgenstein saves the independence of the second "godhead" mentioned in the epigraph of this chapter.[18] While Fichte was convinced that the world can be transformed according to the designs of the rational self, Wittgenstein was convinced of the futility of this vision, and of the absolute powerlessness of the self. With respect to both the rule of reason, and the self-determination of individuals, the worldview of the *Tractatus* is one of a determined rejection of the aspirations of the Enlightenment.

That Wittgenstein should have such a conception of the self is not entirely surprising. The previous remark was written in the middle of World War I, an event which shook to the core the hitherto dominant opinion that history and nature could be subjected to a rational human will. The war, with its unheard-of destruction, accompanied by astounding failures of diplomacy, and military decisions which were as ruthless as they were incompetent, revealed how helplessly dependent people had become on the very forces and organizations which were supposed to insure their power and control. Some pessimistic thinkers, such as Schopenhauer and Nietzsche, had made such views known before the twentieth century and its first massive catastrophe. The discrepancy between the technological power and the wisdom of Western civilization had not escaped the more perceptive writers of the Victorian age. But the war, with its unprecedented numbers of casualties, brought home to the majority of people how badly the ideals of the Enlightenment had failed. After World War I, the general mood and attitude of intellectuals turned from confidence in progress and human emancipation to a profound feeling of futility and helplessness. Pettiness, incompetence, and corruption became increasingly evident in the very bodies that made the decisions for the millions, often with the most disastrous consequences. The modern world began to be seen as irremediably absurd. The experience of World War I laid the groundwork for the philosophy and literature of Existentialism, in which the basic alienation of the self from the world emerged as the dominant theme. In the light of such historical events as World War I, the aspirations of the Enlightenment were bound to look antiquated and naive. It could be argued, in other words, that Wittgenstein, in his remarks about the self, simply expressed what plainly lay in view at the time.

One aspect of Wittgenstein's thought may appear surprising at first sight. Wittgenstein conceives of the self as a radically diminished entity, as a subject that has absolutely no role to play in the world, but at the same time he gives support to what seems the very opposite philosophical position, namely Solipsism. Wittgenstein's position, as outlined so far, implies that the self is nothing, Solipsism maintains that the self is everything, that nothing exists besides the self. In section 5.62 of the *Tractatus,* Wittgenstein writes:

> For what the solipsist *means* is quite correct; only it cannot be *said,* but makes itself manifest. The world is *my* world: this is manifest in the fact that the limits of language (of the language which alone I understand) mean the limits of *my* world.[19]

Some of the implications of this remark are, again, shown by related remarks from the *Notebooks:*

What has history to do with me? Mine is the first and only world!
I want to report how *I* found the world. What others in the world have
told me about the world is a very small and incidental part of my
experience in the world. *I* have to judge the world, to measure things.[20]

The philosophical justifications for this kind of egocentrism can be
elucidated as follows. In 5.6, Wittgenstein states: "The limits of my
language mean the limits of my world." This does not mean that I may be
ignorant of certain aspects of reality because I lack a certain vocabulary
(for example, the vocabulary and the concepts of quantum physics).
There is always the possibility of increasing my vocabulary and my
knowledge. The limits of language to which Wittgenstein refers are the
logical limits, for the *logical* limits of language can never be transcended.
It is in principle impossible to meaningfully speak of such things as
"round squares," "married bachelors," or Lewis Carroll's "grin of the
Cheshire cat" (a grin which supposedly lingers on even after mouth and
face have vanished). To "speak" of such things is tantamount to
producing nonsense (and the point of Lewis Carroll's episode is, of
course, to produce delightful nonsense).
    But the logical limits of language are also the limits of the world. It is
not only impossible to *talk* meaningfully about "married bachelors," but
it is also impossible for such entities to exist. Even the boldest
imagination would be stalled if it had to imagine a married bachelor, or a
grin without a mouth. Illogical things are impossible in the strictest sense
of the word—they could not exist even in theory. Thus Wittgenstein
concludes that the limits of logic and the limits of reality are the same.
"Logic pervades the world: the limits of the world are also its limits."[21]
    To show the absoluteness of the limits of logic, i.e., their strict
inviolability, one can compare them with other kinds of limits, namely
with those set by the laws of physics, for example. In practice, physical
limits cannot be transcended either, but one can at least *imagine* a
science fiction world in which pigs fly by flapping their ears, where rivers
run uphill, or where people grow always younger, until they vanish in a
womb. It is possible to construct certain realities other than the one
which actually exists. But no author of science fiction, no matter how
imaginative, will be able to transgress the laws of logic. If such an author
talked about a strange planet where there are "married bachelors" or
"grins without mouths," one simply would not understand what the
author is talking about. And if people said they can "imagine" such things,

their utterances would remain literally without meaning. Whenever one thinks, speaks, imagines, or understands at all, one inevitably moves within the limits of logic.[22]

The laws of logic are always enacted by *my* thinking or speaking. Even if other people speak or think, the identification of what they are doing presupposes that *I* understand them, i.e., that *I* think. It is *my* language and its logic which I am not able to transcend, and the world which is pervaded by this logic is thus *my* world. It is the world which I cannot leave. I cannot imagine other worlds, for whatever I can imagine is thereby subject to the laws of logic, and thus already part of my world. Hence, the truth of Solipsism.

What is important for Solipsism is the fact that there is no boundary between my world and other worlds. There is only one world, and this world is (in the sense explained) *my* world. The oneness of this world explains why there is no incompatibility between Wittgenstein's contention that the self is not part of the world, and his other contention that there is truth in Solipsism. The two contentions are, in fact, identical. For in neither case is the self a being *in* the world. The contention discussed earlier holds that only body and psyche are part of the world, while the true self is outside, being the "limit" of the world. The self of the Solipsist thesis is also not part of the world, but the enactor of the laws of logic, i.e., of the limit of the world. Thus, there is on the one hand the world without even a trace of the subject, and on the other hand the self in complete separation from everything empirical or worldly. Wittgenstein writes in the *Tractatus:*

Here it can be seen that solipsism, when its implications are followed out strictly, coincides with pure realism. The self of solipsism shrinks to a point without extension, and there remains the reality co-ordinated with it.[23]

*

The radical separation of the self from the world also finds expression in the theory of the "fact-value gap" discussed in Chapter II. To say that "all facts are on the same level"[24] implies that the self cannot expect any guidance from the facts. If all facts are equally important or unimportant, if they are neutral with respect to any values, then their study or contemplation will not furnish any unquestionable maxims on how to act or live. And to say that *"how* things are in the world is a matter of

complete indifference for what is higher"[25] implies that such things that
are traditionally known as "being a good person," or "to make the world a
better place to live in," are irrelevant to the development or realization of
the self. That "God does not reveal himself in the world"[26] also means that
the innermost self cannot express itself in the external world.

It is clear that for this utterly alienated self, the traditional guidance by
God and a church is not possible. The self is entirely dependent on its
own resources to create a design for living: "If the good or bad exercise
of the will does alter the world, it can alter only the limits of the world,
not the facts—not what can be expressed by means of language."[27] To
alter the limits of the world means foremost to change the self itself, the
"metaphysical subject."[28] This does not mean that matters of ethics are
"subjective" in the sense of being functions of one's personal instincts
and emotions, for one's emotional reactions to the events of the world
are just more facts, and these facts stand as much in need of an ultimate,
absolute evaluation as any other facts.[29] (There is, in any event, no
compelling reason for assuming that personal feelings are a better judge
of events than are the norms of society or any other traditional moral
authority.) To locate the difference between good and bad in the
innermost self, the "metaphysical subject," means to tie this difference to
the way in which the world is seen as a *whole.* The difference between
good and bad is not given in the form of a criterion by which one can
separate the morally acceptable facts from those which are morally
reprehensible, but in the way in which *all* facts are perceived by the self,
including the facts of one's personal feelings and reactions.

In section 6.421 of the *Tractatus,* Wittgenstein says that "Ethics is
transcendental." The word "transcendental" is used, again, in the Kantian
sense, indicating that ethics (like logic) is a "form" through which one
perceives things. As a person who wears green glasses will inevitably see
everything in shades of green, so the very perception of facts will,
according to Wittgenstein, be either entirely good or entirely bad:

> In short, the effect [of the fact that the good will alters the *limits* of the
> world, not the world itself] must be that it becomes an altogether
> different world. It must, so to speak, wax and wane as a whole.
> The world of the happy man is a different one from that of the unhappy
> man.[30]

The world seen with the eyes of a happy person is morally good, the
world seen with those of an unhappy person bad.[31] While in Kant's

philosophy, however, the "forms" of perception are in some sense absolute, Wittgenstein suggests that it is a matter of one's own will to perceive the world as a whole in one way or the other. Thus he commands: "Live happily!"[32], and as has been mentioned earlier, asserts that a happy person is one who sees the world *sub specie aeterni,* i.e., with the profoundly disinterested eyes of an aesthete.[33] Time and again Wittgenstein's reflections come back to the idea that it is the artist's way of perceiving facts which ultimately ought to be aimed at:

> Is it the artistic way of looking at things, that it looks at the world with a happy eye?— "Life is serious, while art is serene."[34]

> But we could say: The happy life seems to be in some way more *harmonious* than the unhappy.[35] And if I now ask myself: But why should I live happily, then this of itself seems to me to be a tautological question; the happy life seems to be justified of itself, it seems that it *is* the only right life.[36]

The radical inwardness of ethics conceived by Wittgenstein has its counterpart in most of the reflections on ethics that can be found in the philosophical treatises and literary works of Existentialism, the school of thought which dominated a great deal of twentieth century philosophy. As different as Wittgenstein's writings are from those of the Existentialists, they both deal with a conception of self which exhibits a most extreme form of alienation, and a most radical separation of the individual from society and the world.

The situation with which the Existentialists try to cope is the perceived breakdown of all traditional values, meanings, and orientations. With such foundations of morality as religion, tradition, communal conventions, or authoritative legal systems gone, the self finds itself in a situation of "abandonment," obliged to create its own value system out of its own resources. In view of the absence of all pre-established rules and goals, the self is in a permanent state of "anguish," as it has to make the most crucial decisions on the basis of nothing.

Jean-Paul Sartre's reflections in his essay "Existentialism is a Humanism" (1946) are typical of this kind of thinking. Sartre mentions the development which had taken place: The moral system of traditional Christianity had broken down, and secular theoreticians, in the tradition of the Enlightenment, had tried to construct a value system without metaphysical authorities, a system based on the facts of nature alone.

Sartre rejects such a secular morality as invalid (declaring facts to be irrelevant for the establishment of morality in the same way Wittgenstein had done so). With the demise of God as a moral authority, according to Sartre, *everything* is lost:

> The existentialist, on the contrary, finds it extremely embarrassing that God does not exist, for there disappears with Him all possibility of finding values in an intelligible heaven. There can no longer be any good *a priori*, . . . Dostoevsky once wrote 'If God did not exist, everything would be permitted'; and that, for existentialism, is the starting point. Everything is indeed permitted if God does not exist, and man is in consequence forlorn, for he cannot find anything to depend upon either within or outside himself.[37]

The phrase "within himself" refers to such things as feelings or instincts. Neither Sartre nor Wittgenstein believed that one's personal emotions are a valid substitute for a universally valid value system: "The existentialist does not believe in the power of passion . . . He thinks that man is responsible for his passion."[38] Passions are just facts, facts with regard to which the self can have a number of possible attitudes. Facts by themselves do not determine what attitude one should have toward them. The determination of what is good and bad is the task of the self which is radically independent of, and in principle removed from, the facts of the world.

The doctrine in which the self's independence of facts is summarized is the statement that "existence precedes essence."[39] It is a doctrine which is directed against the idea of a "human nature." The Enlightenment tradition had assumed that human beings had a factually determined nature with identifiable needs, inclinations, limited possibilities, and thus inherent standards of what is good or bad for them. For example, a political system which keeps the majority of citizens in physical misery, is bad, while a system of mores which is free of socially unnecessary sexual repression is good. The facts of the natural human constitution are considered to be highly relevant for the establishment of values, as far as Enlightenment thinkers are concerned. Sartre denies any such relevancy. Like other Existentialists he insists that no matter what the natural human constitution may be, it is in principle always possible to have a number of plausible attitudes toward it. One may follow, as it were, the lead of nature, but one may also suppress all natural instincts. What a person does in this matter is his or her free decision. The way human beings are (their "essence") does not prescribe how they are to live. The fact *that* they live ("existence") always precedes *how* they live.

This conception of a self that is radically separated not only from communities, traditions, and legal systems, but also from the feelings, instincts, and physical needs of its own empirical embodiment, can be considered the characteristic result of twentieth century thinking. It is common to such different philosophies as that of Wittgenstein's *Tractatus* and Sartre's Existentialism. Furthermore, it also pervades the imagination of modern writers, painters, choreographers, and film makers. It is the plausible product of a world in which the ingenuity and productivity of humanity has reached unprecedented extremes, but where this man-made world of things has gone out of control, overpowering its makers as an alien force of frightening proportions.

Yeats: "An Irish Airman Foresees His Death"

William Butler Yeats was born in 1865 near Dublin. At age twenty-one, he published his first book of poetry, went to London, and began to participate vigorously in the literary life of the 1890s. His orientation was cosmopolitan, but he engaged himself in promoting Irish literature. His ideal was poetry which is English in words, but Irish in spirit. In 1904, he founded the Abbey Theatre in Dublin. Its affairs often entangled him in the conflict between the demands of Irish nationalists and the British authorities. Because of such experiences, at times he felt extremely alienated from his native country. In 1922, he became a Senator of the newly created Irish Free State, and he continued in his attempts to revitalize a national Irish tradition. He spent the last years of his life in Italy and France, and he died near Nice in 1939.

The poem below was written in 1919.[40]

AN IRISH AIRMAN FORESEES HIS DEATH

I know that I shall meet my fate
Somewhere among the clouds above;
Those that I fight I do not hate,
Those that I guard I do not love;
My country is Kiltartan Cross,
My countrymen Kiltartan's poor,
No likely end could bring them loss

Or leave them happier than before.
Nor law, nor duty bade me fight,
Nor public men, nor cheering crowds,
A lonely impulse delight
Drove to this tumult in the clouds;
I balanced all, brought all to mind,

The years to come seemed waste of breath,
A waste of breath the years behind
In balance with this life, this death.

Coincidentally, the theme of the poem may bear a certain relationship to Wittgenstein's participation in World War I. Little has been published about that aspect of Wittgenstein's life. Wittgenstein joined the Austrian army as a volunteer at the beginning of the war, and his conduct brought him several promotions and decorations for bravery. But it is hard to imagine that he would have been part of the chauvinism and partisan hysteria which seized the warring nations in 1914. Such things as his student years in Cambridge, and his friendship with David Pinsent (who fell in the war, and to whose memory the *Tractatus* is dedicated) makes it unlikely that Wittgenstein saw in the military actions the meaning that politicians and the newspapers attributed to them.[41] That Wittgenstein apparently hoped to put an honorable end to his life goes a lot further toward explaining his conduct at the front than such things as plain patriotism.[42]

Yeats' poem is not particularly modern in any way except with respect to its outlook on life. It has regular rhymes, syntactical order, and it states its message plainly. It describes the situation of a man who is completely alienated from the world and his role in it. Externally the protagonist is engaged in the affairs of the world to the point where he sacrifices his life for the purpose of achieving victory for his side. But the enemy against whom he fights is not really his enemy, and the country for which he will die is not really his home. He only goes through the external motions of allegiance and hostile action, but the person who is doing these things is not really his self. His true self is not part of this world at all.

The airman's absence from the world is also expressed by the perceived uselessness of his action: it does not make any difference to the community of his origin whether he succeeds in anything or not, or whether he lives or dies. As far as the poor of Kiltartan are concerned, he is a nonentity. Compared with ancient communities, where warriors were personally known, their deeds closely observed, and their memory woven into the myths and stories of the people, the modern community has lost any organic and plausible connection with those who may accomplish outstanding deeds.

The airman's entire life is without purpose, because it is not embedded in the network of virtues and duties which governed the conduct of men of former ages. The reason why he fights at all is explained by an inexplicable "impulse," a motivation which is not connected with anything in his own or other people's lives. It is an extreme case of living timelessly, of cutting one's self off from every past and future. It is an unworldly life.

That the flyer's death will occur in the air is, apart from biographical reasons,[43] an indication of the protagonist's unworldliness. As a professional flyer he already lives, as it were, outside of the world. But, as in other experiences of the impossibility of transcendence, there is no indication that this unworldliness implies residency in another, transcendent world. The sky alludes to heaven, but only as a means to indicate the limits of the world. The airman's death is not a departure, but an end. His homelessness is complete.

Musil: *The Man Without Qualities*

Robert Musil was born in Klagenfurt, Austria in 1886. He studied civil engineering and philosophy. After some years at University and in public administration, however, he turned to full-time writing. He lived in Berlin and Vienna. In 1938, when Germany annexed Austria, he emigrated to Switzerland. His monumental and innovative novel, *The Man Without Qualities,* was published in sections between 1931 and 1943. In spite of its length of well over a thousand pages it is a fragment. Musil died in 1942 in Geneva.

The Man Without Qualities is the story of Ulrich, an Austrian who lives through the inner disintegration of the Hapsburg Empire. This disintegration is seen as inevitable. It represents, in fact, the dissolution of the Victorian age before the onslaught of the twentieth century and its revolutionizing tendencies. The demise of the Old World signals the disappearance of order, stability, hierarchies of authority, established value systems, set expectations and purposes, and a sense of belonging. Ulrich, the witness to the disintegration of the brittle Empire, is already a modern man: he is without serious attachments, traditional principles, or idealogical affiliations. He is nowhere at home. He has a certain lifestyle, but that style is accidental; it does not indicate any commitment or basic conviction. He identifies with nothing: he is a Man Without Qualities.

The following passages are from one of the early chapters of *The Man Without Qualities*.[44] The described event is set in 1913, one year before the outbreak of the war which was to bring about the external disintegration of the Hapsburg Empire. Ulrich has just returned from abroad to finally settle down in his country of origin. His thoughts concerning the decoration of his residence reveal the basic rootlessness which is the fate of modern man as conceived by Musil.

ULRICH

When he built his house and had occupancy, as the Bible puts it, Ulrich had an experience for which, in a way, he had been waiting. He found himself in the enviable position of having to remodel his residence from scratch—in absolutely any way he saw fit. From a stylistically faithful restoration to total recklessness, all possibilities of architecture were at his disposal, and his mind was free to choose among every known style, from that of the Ancient Assyrians to Cubism. So, what was he to choose? Modern man is born in a clinic, and he dies in a clinic. Hence he ought to live in a clinic as well! This demand had recently been formulated by one of the leading architects, and a reformer of interior architecture had demanded movable walls for all apartments, on the grounds that men had to learn to trust each other by living closely together, rather than isolating themselves from each other. In those days a new time had begun (for that it does constantly), and a new time needs a new style. Luckily for Ulrich, the little palais, in the condition in which he found it, had already three different styles built on top of each other, and it was impossible to do all the things which he was supposed to do. Still, the responsibility of having to decide on how to shape and furnish his house weighed heavily on him . . .

Well, the Man Without Qualities, who had already taken the first step of returning to the country of his origin, also took the second step to insure that it would be external forces that shaped his life: he left the decoration of his residence to the inspiration of the appropriate decorator shops, convinced that they would take care of preserving all proper traditions, prejudices, and limitations. He himself re-did only some of the old-fashioned items that were already in place—the deer antlers in the whitewashed hallway, or the reinforced ceiling of the drawing room. Apart from that he simply added whatever struck him as practical or convenient.

Usually a style expresses a mind-set: an attitude toward life, a basic orientation, guiding values. The difference of style in the art and architecture of the Egyptians and the Greeks, for example, expresses a difference of outlook and way of life, and it is close to unthinkable that a people like the Ancient Greeks could have built Egyptian pyramids and temples. It seems natural, then, that the successive stages of the development of humanity are expressed in a succession of distinctive styles, and that the people of every historical epoch can be at home only in the world which they create for themselves according to their own values. Modern humanity, according to this understanding, had to develop its own style, its own way of building and furnishing its living places. That is what the remark concerning the "clinical" style of modern architecture refers to, and what such innovative architects as Adolf Loos and Walter Gropius had advocated since the first decade of the twentieth century.

Ulrich's place in this sequence of styles and ways of life is not with the modernism of the twentieth century. His reference to modern architecture is as sneering and ironic as that to any other style and tradition. Ulrich does not identify with the mind-set of the cultural innovators; modernism is as alien to him as the culture of the Ancients. His peculiar situation is to subscribe to no style or mind-set whatsoever, to be a stranger in any possible culture. There is no possible external expression of what he stands for, because he stands for nothing. His style is to have no style. His self is a "point without extension."[45]

Since Ulrich lives, he has to attach himself to *some* externals, but these are strictly accidental. Since for Ulrich all styles are on the same level, and since he has no compelling criteria by which to choose one style over any other, he has to leave such things as decoration and furniture to chance and accident. He ends up with a certain environment, but this environment is not an expression of his inner life. He is as unattached to the actual style (or styles) of his residence as he is to that of the ancient Assyrians. And his country is not really his country, his roots are not really his roots, his house is not really his home. In an important sense he does not have a place to stay. Nothing he does is ultimately characteristic of *him;* there is no feature which defines his proper self. Ulrich's self has no proper identity, it is a self without existence.

Rimbaud: "The Drunken Ship"

Jean Arthur Rimbaud was born in a small town in Northern France in 1854. He began to write poetry at the age of fifteen. At the age of seventeen, he began to write poems which were so innovative that until the twentieth century, few people could understand or appreciate them. In retrospect it can be said that Rimbaud was one of the inventors of modern poetry. Decades before most other writers took such risks, Rimbaud violated not only the canon of traditional poetical forms, but wrote texts which left behind narrative cohesiveness, identifiable selves, understandable statements, and logical order. Many of his prose poems of the early 1870s were already "abstract" in the sense that certain kinds of twentieth century painting were abstract. Needless to say, Rimbaud did not gain any recognition as a poet at the time, except from a few friends. One of the few literati who did take an interest in his work was his friend Verlaine.

Much of the darkness of Rimbaud's poetry results from his attempt to break out of ordinary reality and to reach the "unknown" (an attempt which was repeated more systematically by the Surrealists, who considered Rimbaud as one of their principal forerunners). In a letter of 1871, Rimbaud writes:

Right now, I'm depriving myself as much as I can. Why? I want to be a poet, and I am working at making myself a *visionary:* you won't understand at all, and I'm not even sure I can explain it to you. The problem is to attain the unknown by disorganizing *all the senses.*[46]

And in another letter of the same year he states:

I say you have to be a visionary, make yourself a visionary. A poet makes himself a visionary through a long, boundless, and systematized *disorganization of all the senses*[47] . . . so Baudelaire is the first visionary, the king of poets, *a real God.* And still he lived in too artistic a milieu; and his highly praised form is silly. The inventions of the unknown demand new forms.[48]

The French word which is translated here as "visionary" is "voyant," which can also be translated as "seer," or "prophet." Rimbaud obviously refers to those people in ancient and primitive societies who served as the spokespersons of their gods, as their soothsayers, or their shamans. Rimbaud meant to emulate their trance-inducing techniques in a conscious, methodical way. In this sense, he thought of the poet as the "Supreme Scientist! For he attains the unknown,"[49] and as a person who experiments like "a man grafting warts onto his face and growing them there."[50] The methodically induced "disorganization of the senses" leads to the chaotic juxtaposition of times, places, and objects which characterizes much of Rimbaud's poetry. It also leads to the dissolution of that sense of self which is considered normal in Western civilization, and which has to be subverted, according to Rimbaud, to attain a truer perception of reality.

At the age of nineteen Rimbaud, for all practical purposes, gave up writing and left France. For eighteen years he lived first in Aden, and then in Ethiopia, where he tried to make enough money to retire in his homeland. While in Africa, he contracted a disease which forced him to return to France, and to have his leg amputated. He died in the hospital in Marsailles in 1891.

Rimbaud wrote "The Drunken Ship" at the age of seventeen. The original[51] is written in rhymed verse, as are all the earlier poems. The imagery, however, begins to show the signs of willful disintegration which his "seer letters" demand, and which is cultivated to the extreme in his later poems.

THE DRUNKEN SHIP

As I went down the indifferent rivers
I felt free of the guiding ropes of the haulers:
Screaming redskins had used the men as their targets,
And nailed them naked to painted stakes.

I did not care about the crew—
Haulers of Flemish wheat or English cloth.
When all this was finished, the haulers gone,
The riverflow let me drift as I wished.

I raced through furiously splashing tides—
All winter long—more stubborn than the brains of a child.
And never did severed peninsulas ever
Go under in more triumphant turmoil.

Storms gave their blessing to my maritime wakings,
I danced on the water lighter than cork.
Ten nights, called the eternal rollers of victims,
Without caring about the dull eye of the lighthouse . . .

Sweeter than a tart apple is to a child
Green water washed through my hull of pine,
Washing away the stains of blue wine
And vomit, and tearing rudder and anchor away.

And from then on I bathed in the poem
Of oceans, churning, and infused by the light of the stars,
Devouring sky-blue greens, where, delighted and pale,
At times a pensively looking dead man descends:

Where, suddenly tinting the blue, deliria
And slow rhythms under the stroking light of day,
Stronger than drink, and vaster than your music,
The bitter reds of love ferment!

I know the skies, bursting with flashes, and the gushing
And the surfs and the currents: the evening I know,
And the dawn as glittering as a swarm of doves.
And sometimes I've seen what people think they saw.

I have seen the low sun, stained with mystic horrors.
Illuminated with long, purple clots,
Resembling actors of ancient plays,
The waves that roll far off their flickering blinds.

I have dreamed the green nights of dazzling snows.
The kisses, mounting slowly to the eyes of the sea.
The circulation of unheard-of saps.
And the waking, yellow and blue of phosphorus singing.

Whole months I followed, like stampeding cattle.
The swells in their assault on the reefs.
Not knowing that the glowing feet of the Marys
Could force the puffing snout of the seas.

I found, you know, incredible Floridas:
Panthers in human skins, their eyes among the flowers,
And rainbows stretched like bridle reins
To blue-green herds under the sea's horizon.

I saw enormous swamps ferment, and traps
With a whole Leviathan rotting in the reeds!
And falling waters in quiet zones.
And distances crashing into the abyss.

Glaciers, suns of silver, waves of pearls, embroidered skies!
Ugly debris at the end of brown gulfs,
Here giant serpents, devoured by insects,
Fall from gnarled trees with dark scents.

I would have liked to show the children these Dorados
Of the blue wave, the fish of gold, the singing fish
—Flower foams rocked by drifting, and
Indescribable winds have winged me at times.

And at times I was like a martyr, tired of poles and zones,
And the sea, whose sobbing made gentle my rolling,
Brought up her shadowy flowers, studded with bright-yellow suckers.
And so I remained, on my knees, like a woman . . .

Almost an island, rocking on my railings the fights
And the shit of noisy, yellow-eyed birds.
And on I rolled, while through my rotten ropes
The drowned sank backward to their sleep.

Now I, lost ship in the hair of the reefs,
Thrown by storms into birdless skies,
I, whom neither men-of-war nor Hansa ships
Could rescue, water-drunk carcass that I am,

Free, letting out smoke and purple fogs,
I, crashing through the reddening wall of the sky,
Which is covered—delicious jam for good poets!—
With lichens of sunlight and azure slime,

I, who ran, stained with electric moons,
Like a crazy plank (seahorses, black ones, go with me),
While Julys were clubbing the ultramarine
Skies of funnels ablaze,

I, who trembled, hearing at fifty leagues off
The horny groan of thick Maelstroms Behemoths,
I, the homeless roamer of azure immobilities,
I do miss Europe's ancient, narrow walls!

I've seen sidereal archipelagos! And islands,
Whose toxic skies are open to the traveler:
Is it in these boundless nights, in which you sleep,
O future power—exiled, like countless golden birds?

I've tried too long. The dawns do break my heart,
The sun is bitter, and the moon is an atrocity.
Acrid love has swollen me with drunken stupors.
I wish my keel would burst and I would vanish in the sea!

If I desired any European water, it would be the puddle,
Cold and black, where in the fragrance-loaded dusk
A squatting, melancholy child lets go
A boat as fragile as a butterfly in May.

No longer can I, bathed in your gentle languor, waves,
Follow the routes of carriers of merchandise,
Nor go for boasting flags and fireworks,
Nor navigate beneath the evil eyes of pontoon bridges.

The journey of the ship is one from civilization to a fantastic, primordial world. And since the ship itself is a product of civilized labor, the movement of the vessel is accompanied by its progressive disintegration. At the end of the poem the human world has vanished, and the ship has dissolved into its natural elements.

The poem begins with the ship being hauled through canalized rivers, carrying the goods of a commerce-oriented culture. The haulers' ropes are indicative of the ship's ties to civilization. Then a race not acculturated to this kind of civilization puts an end to the ship's utilitarian existence and lets it drift with the natural flow of the river. (Rimbaud evokes the nineteenth century stereotypes of the "savages." But while the actions of these "redskins" were feared and despised by most members of Western civilization, Rimbaud welcomes them as acts of liberation.)

The ship ends up in the untamed ocean, rejoicing in the total absence of civilized restraints. The lighthouse, a distant reminder of the practical, technologically adept ways of Western civilization, is not greeted with hope for rescue, but indifference. The ship's rudder is torn away: the guidance of its fate is now forever taken away from rational deliberation, and handed over to the uncontrolled forces of nature.

Strange continents and archipelagos come in sight. The ship begins to be a piece of nature itself: as its parts are washed away, birds use it as if it were a rock or an island. Finally, its "carcass" is washed up on a reef. The final dissolution is welcomed as a relief.

The last two stanzas mention Europe again. The only appeal of this continent's "narrowness" are the children, i.e., those inhabitants who have not yet been fully acculturated into the civilization of merchandise ("carriers of cotton"), nationalism ("flags and flames"), and nature-defying structures ("evil pontoon bridges"). But on the whole that ancient continent is a place where it is impossible to live, where no acceptable form of existence can be found. Western civilization has become a dead end. The last lines of the poem confirm that the loss of self represented by the ship's journey is the only option left.

The dissolution of the self which is represented by the "Drunken Ship" is not the kind of loss and homelessness represented by Musil's *Man Without Qualities,* for example, but rather an experience of liberation or self-fulfillment. The ship's disintegration into the untamed forces of nature represent a unification (or reunification) with a larger cosmos which, according to Rimbaud's thinking, has been unduly suppressed and ignored by Western civilization, if not by all human cultures. This larger cosmos appears in a two-fold form, as external nature with its untamed elements, and as the irrational part of the human soul. What is directly represented in "The Drunken Ship" is the least controlled of the natural elements, water. Carl Gustav Jung saw water as a symbol for the Unconscious, the irrational part of mind that is always ready to flood and submerge the artifices of consciousness and reason. Rimbaud, writing long before Jung, gave a clear indication in his "seer" letters that the poet made an attempt to connect with those parts of the soul which are beyond the control of the will and rational planning. Rimbaud does, in fact, go so far as to claim that the real self is not at all located in the conscious, civilized mind, but in a depth to which one can only passively listen:

> They [the Romantics] illustrate perfectly the fact that the song is very rarely the work of the singer . . . For *I* is somebody else. If brass wakes as a bugle, it is not its fault at all. That is quite clear to me: I am a spectator at the flowering of my thought: I watch it, I listen to it: I draw a bow across a string: a symphony stirs in the depths, or surges onto the stage.[52]

The loss of the conscious, civilized self, in other words, is ultimately no loss at all, but part of a process of becoming authentic in a way in which most civilized people fail to be authentic. The dissolution of the self in "The Drunken Ship" is a welcome reversal of the self-alienation which is afflicting Western man.

"The Drunken Ship" and Rimbaud's reflections have obvious parallels in the work of other pioneers of modern thought. Sigmund Freud's investigations of the unconscious mind are a case in point. The significance of Freud's work for modern culture lies primarily in using the tools of science to show that the behavior of people is not motivated and inspired by reason and the precepts of civilization alone, but by the promptings of unknown wishes, old fears, powerful and primitive instincts, etc. The real self, according to Freud in the following quote, is not the Ego, which just manages, so to speak, the limited and identifiable demands and affairs of the day, but the largely unconscious Id whose powers and visions appear primarily when the conscious mind is at rest, i.e., in dreams, trances, under the influence of drugs, or in a state of hypnosis. As Rimbaud in his poem, Freud at times conceives of a mode of self-realization which consists in giving up the boundaries of the Ego set by rational calculation and the civil attempt to control nature:

> Or, to put it more correctly, originally the ego includes everything, later it separates off an external world from itself. Our present ego-feeling is, therefore, only a shrunken residue of a much more inclusive—indeed, an all-embracing—feeling which corresponded to a more intimate bond between the ego and the world about it. If we may assume that there are many people in whose mental life this primary ego-feeling has persisted to a greater or less degree, it would exist in them side by side with the narrower and more sharply demarcated ego-feeling of maturity, like a kind of counterpart to it. In that case, the

ideational contents appropriate to it would be precisely those of limitlessness and of a bond with the universe— the same ideas with which my friend [Romain Roland] elucidated the 'oceanic' feeling.[53]

The previous quote of Freud's concerning the self and the Unconscious have some striking similarities to those of Nietzsche in his *The Birth of Tragedy,* and the conception of the "Dionysian" in this book, in turn, bears a close resemblance to Rimbaud's "Drunken Ship." Nietzsche's book was written during the same time period in which Rimbaud wrote the "Drunken Ship," although the two authors, of course, were unaware of each other. One of its decisive ideas is that poetry, as all great art, is not so much made, but emerges out of the irrational depths of the soul. In chapter five of *The Birth of Tragedy* Nietzsche stresses the passivity of the ego as much as Rimbaud does in his letters. As a creator, the artist does not live in the world of logic, reason, control, consciousness, and clearly delineated, separate beings, but is, rather, united, in a "Dionysian drunkenness" or "frenzy," with the limitless and irrational forces that underly ordinary reality. In this prerational and precivilized state the artist gains those insights into the ultimate nature of the world which makes his or her works significant for the rest of humanity.

Nietzsche's early work, as that of Freud and indeed all of European thought of the time, was profoundly influenced by Schopenhauer's conception of the self as "Will." Schopenhauer's widely read *The World as Will and Representation* prepared the European intelligentsia not only for a general irrational conception of life (as has been pointed out in Chapter II), but also specifically for a conception of the self which stresses the importance of the Id with respect to the Ego, to use psychoanalytic terminology. In Schopenhauer's thinking the very conception of an ego as distinct and separate from the rest of the world is something like an illusion. Using the language of Indian religion as well as his version of Kantian transcendentalism, Schopenhauer describes all identifiable entities, objects as well as persons, as mere appearances ("Representations") which in reality are nothing but fleeting aspects of one all-embracing and indivisible Will. Thus, strictly speaking, there are no egos or individuals in the first place, and such experiences as the "Drunken Ship's" disintegration have no destructiveness about them, but are the realization of what basically is the case. The vanishing of the self, according to this thinking, is nothing but the disappearance of a chimera.

The entire tradition of Irrationalism, which began to emerge in the thought of the nineteenth century, and which culminated in the critique of the rational Ego in the writings of thinkers such as Nietzsche, has a significant relationship to one of the major political ideologies of the twentieth century, Fascism. While it would be incorrect to attribute fascist goals to writers such as Nietzsche, there is no doubt that right-wing intellectuals (such as Gottfried Benn or Marinetti) drew continuous inspiration from the above tradition, and thus revealed a practical dimension of Irrationalism which has made a closer examination of its basic tenets imperative.

Broch: From *The Sleepwalkers*

Hermann Broch was born in Vienna in 1886. He is one of the most important and least known authors of modern literature in German. In the course of his writing career he developed the idea of the "multidimensional novel," an attempt to incorporate into narrative fiction not only the traditional subject matters of the human world, but the biological and metaphysical levels of existence as well. The work which deals specifically with the modern world is his trilogy, *The Sleepwalkers,* which he wrote in Vienna during 1928-1931. The first novel, *Pasenow or Romanticism,* is set in 1888. The second, *Esch or Anarchy,* in 1903, and the third, *Hugenau or Objectivity,* in 1818. The characters of the novels overlap in part. Together they describe, in connection with exemplary lives, the disintegration of the old European world, and the emergence of modernism as Broch perceived it. Broch emigrated to the United States in 1940. He died in New Haven, Connecticut in 1951.

The following excerpt is taken from *Pasenow or Romanticism.* Pasenow is a *Junker* and officer in the Prussian army. The sarcastic description of the role of the uniform in his life reveals the sense of order and the fear of anarchy which characterized much of the old European world.

THE UNIFORM[54]

. . . for it is the true purpose of the uniform to demonstrate and maintain order, and to counteract the dissolving and fluctuating tendencies of life—in the same way in which it hides the softness of the human body, a man's underwear, and a man's skin. It is for good reasons that a soldier on guard duty has to wear white gloves. Thus the man who in the morning has closed the last button of his uniform has received a second and less penetrable skin, and he returns, as it were, to his truer and more stable existence. Secluded in his hard casing, locked up by means of straps and clamps, he begins to forget his underwear and the insecurities of life. In fact, life itself moves somewhat away from him. When he has pulled down the lower seam of his military coat so that no wrinkles are left on the surfaces of breast and back, then even the child, which he loves, and the wife, in whose embrace he has conceived the child, have moved so far away into the civilian distance that he hardly recognizes the mouth which his wife offers him for a goodbye kiss, and his own home becomes something strange, something which one is not really supposed to visit in uniform. And when he walks in his uniform to the barracks or to his office in the administration, then it is not arrogance which makes him ignore the civilians. It is rather that he cannot comprehend anymore that there is something beneath those alien and barbarian covers which has anything to do with the humanity which he himself experiences. But this does not mean that the man in uniform is blind or prejudiced, as is often assumed. He is still a human being like you or me. He thinks about eating and sex, and he reads his newspaper over breakfast. But he is not really connected with things anymore. And since things are not close to him, he is able to categorize them according to good and evil. For intolerance and lack of understanding are the true foundations of security in life.

The uniform is understood here not as a practical device which allows an easy and quick distinction between friend and foe on the battlefield, but as a symbol of metaphysical proportions. Uniforms have, of course, always had the more than pragmatic connotation of group-solidarity, exclusiveness, and national identity, but with Joachim von Pasenow it gains a significance which reaches into the most basic layers of his life. The attire of the Prussian officer does not simply stand for honor, duty, fatherland in the conventional sense, but for an identifiable existence as such, for an order which renders a man distinct from the threatening and unfathomable chaos of life, the "constant flux" referred to by such philosophers as Heraclitus.

The uniform represents the very opposite of what Rimbaud's "Drunken Ship" stands for, namely the preservation of self, order, distinction, and civilization. Nature, disorder, and self-abandonment are experienced as a threat to everything which distinguishes human beings, from monkeys, amoebas, and other lower forms of life. The price of the realization of what is higher requires incessant vigilance, and necessitates that raw nature be constantly controlled by the imposition of artificial structures on everything which is not a product of culture. This is why the artificial "casing" of the uniform is welcome, and why such things as feelings, sexual intimacy, personal insecurities, and underwear smack of subversion and chaos. And it is the reason why the uniform strikes Pasenow as the proper manifestation of a self.

Yet, ironically, this form of self-preservation results in another form of self-elimination, for the uniform is both practically and symbolically a means to reduce or suppress individuality. Uniforms tend to make people equal in appearance and behaviour, and they indicate that the individual is to be seen as a minor part in a hierarchy or organization which draws attention to itself as a whole, and not as an association in which people function as individual persons. The Prussian administration and military organization in particular were noted for their seemingly incorruptible and efficient functioning as machine-like structures in which personal initiative, compassion, and other expressions of individuality were often ruthlessly suppressed.

The self-preservation which is achieved by the uniform, in other words, results in a rather dubious kind of personal identity, in a mere facade of self. For the self created by the uniform is cut off from everything which could give life and substance to it. It is based on the fear of life, and the inability to live. It is a mistrustful retreat from the forces of nature, not their mastery. For this reason, the praise of the uniform can only be sarcastic. Broch's description of the old European order is one which implicitly makes it clear that that order was bound to collapse from its own hollowness.

Chaplin: *Modern Times*

Charles Spencer Chaplin was born in London in 1889. His parents were music hall entertainers, and Chaplin performed for audiences from an early age. In 1910, he went to the United States, and, beginning in 1913, he performed very successfully in slapstick film comedies. He began to develop his figure of the romantic tramp and social outsider for which he became famous. From 1919 on he worked for his own company, writing, directing, and acting in his own movies. He produced some of the classics of film comedy during the silent movie era: *The Kid* (1923), *Gold Rush*

Figure 6.   Scene from *Modern Times,* (1936)

(1925), and *City Lights* (1931). When sound movies replaced the silent movies in the early 1930s, Chaplin continued producing films without dialogue, still using his special gift for pantomime. In *Modern Times* (1936) speech is pointedly used only via public address systems and mechanical recordings. It was not until his *The Great Dictator* (1940) that Chaplin spoke at all in a movie, and then not until the very end of it.

Chaplin's movies became artistically ever more ambitious, and at the same time increasingly critical of social conditions. Because of the latter, he encountered such massive hostility for alleged Communist sympathies during the McCarthy era, that in 1952 he finally returned to Europe to settle in Switzerland. In England he was knighted in 1975, and he died in Switzerland in 1977.

Modern Times can be described as a fight of the individual self for survival in a modern mass society. Both in its portrayal of the modern work world, and in its treatment of social welfare agencies, the story dramatizes the tendency of modern societies to reduce the individual to a passive and conformist entity which functions exclusively as an anonymous element in a giant apparatus of efficient production and administration. The film develops out of the individualistic resistance of the protagonist, played by Chaplin, and Claire, played by Paulette Goddard, against the overwhelming forces of the modern factory system, police, social administration, and the Great Depression. It ends with an uncertain escape of the couple from these forces.

The film starts with intertwined scenes of herded sheep and crowds of workers rushing to the factories: the movements of people have become as thoughtless and involuntary as those of animals driven to a slaughterhouse. The next scenes show the inside of a modern factory where human beings are dwarfed by giant machines. And the first actions of the protagonist occur along an assembly line where workers perform their monotonous and brainless jobs with an intensity reminiscent of the movement of ants. The scenes make it clear that the machines are not the servants of men, but rather the controllers of the movements of their operators. The workers do not produce according to their own incentives, purpose, and pace, but are mercilessly driven by the rhythm of the assembly line. People are not liberated by advanced technology, but find themselves reduced, as Marx put it, to "appendices of machines."

While the machines of the factory are the immediate controllers of human activity, they themselves are ultimately controlled by the president of the company who supervises the whole process of production by means of a closed circuit television system, and who, like

Orwell's "Big Brother", can talk to any employee at will through a public address system, and who concerns himself primarily with speeding up the assembly lines whenever possible. This president, however, is not a sovereign tyrant, but himself subject to the pressure of competition. He is anxious to out-produce his economic rivals, and thus shows the usual signs of managerial stress, such as the ritual of consuming the daily assortment of pills. The entire system of production, in other words, is shown by the film as an environment in which people have lost control over their lives, in which everything which makes them human is ruthlessly subjected to the ultimate goal of output-maximization. The modern world is presented, in other words, as a situation of extreme and pervasive self-alienation.

Historically, the increased productivity of modern industry was achieved not only by the increased use of machines, but also by the increased regimentation of people at the work place. The artisan was freer than the worker in a shop, and the latter freer than the operator in a mechanized factory. At the time when *Modern Times* was made, the introduction of assembly line production had taken still more initiative away from the worker. Chaplin drew the logical conclusion of this development by introducing the feeding machine into his factory, the device which satirizes most succinctly the dehumanization of modern man.

This machine is tried out in the factory because it promises to give the company the cutting edge over the competition: if it works, the lunch hour can be eliminated. The essence of the machine is that it renders the worker, who is put in a chair where he cannot move, totally passive. In robot-like fashion the contraption serves the worker soup, a main course, and dessert. It also wipes his mouth with an automated napkin. In this way it subjects the very last movements of the worker to an outside-directed mechanism, thus taking the last possibilities of making his own decisions away from him. If being human is defined as being able to make one's own decisions, of directing one's life from within rather than having it controlled from outside, then this feeding machine is the epitome of dehumanization at the working place. It is the ultimate elimination of self-hood.

The event which saves the protagonist of the film from the dehumanizing effects of the modern work world is his nervous breakdown (which results in something like a one-man anarchistic upheaval in the factory), and his escape from the factory. And this way of saving one's self sets the pattern for the whole movie. Time and again the situation arises where the protagonist does not fit into the way things are set up in the modern world, and every time the situation is resolved by the protagonist's wreaking temporary havoc on the status quo, and then vanishing from the scene in flight. In the same way, Claire's undaunted spirit refuses to passively accept either the misery brought on by the Depression, or the bureaucratic dictates of the social services administration and the police. Both the protagonist and Claire save their selves by stubbornly refusing to go along with the dominant patterns of behaviour of the modern world.

The individualism of their rescue shows, of course, that self-hood in modern times seems doomed. Nowhere is there a hint in the movie that collective resistance against the dehumanizing tendencies of the modern world, and thus the abolition of such conditions, is a possibility. The alternatives shown are either conformism or isolated vagrancy. Since the kind of vagrancy tried by the couple is not an option for the millions, the world of *Modern Times* remains what it is: a machinery of production without purpose, an organization without thought and soul, a world without imaginative and autonomous individuals. A world, in other words, in which a genuine self has no place.

Grosz: "The Engineer Heartfield"

George Grosz was born in 1893 in Berlin. He studied art, but the experience of World War I turned him into a militant opponent not only of the militarism and the social order which had made the war possible, but also of any kind of detached aestheticism and "high" culture maintained by the social status quo. Grosz turned from the aesthetics of the art academies to caricatures and highly emotional representations of the victims of war and social oppression. When a politicized version of Dadaism developed in Berlin between 1918 and 1922, Grosz and his friends Helmut and Wieland Herzfelde joined that movement and vigorously furthered its anti-culture and anti-establishment iconoclasm. (As a protest against the boastful and aggressive patriotism cultivated in Germany before and during World War I, Helmut Herzfelde anglicized his name to John Heartfield.)

In the wake of the Russian Revolution of 1917 and the (defeated) German Revolution of 1918, the German Communist Party was founded. Grosz and his friends joined. Grosz' work of that time satirized the militarism, philistinism, and social injustice of modern Germany. By using

Figure 7. George Grosz, *The Engineer Heartfield,* (1920)

the stylistical elements of popular grafitti, he depicted arrogant *Reichswehr* officers, war cripples, haggard workers, lechers, jaded aristocrats, splurging capitalists, humiliated whores, and deranged criminals. Such pictures as Jesus with a World War I gas mask lead to scandals and court actions. Grosz was menaced by outraged viewers so often, that at times he had to hire a body guard. Members of the slowly growing Nazi movement labeled him "the Cultural Bolshevik Number One."

In 1932, Grosz emigrated to the United States, settling in New York City. Because of his past politics, his employment as an art teacher was rather controversial. In 1938, however, he became a citizen, and his art mellowed considerably. In 1959, he returned to Berlin where he died a few weeks after his arrival.

"The Engineer Heartfield" is a mixed water color and collage from 1920, the high point of the Dadaist movement in Berlin. The depicted scene is relatively unified: it has the appearance of a real place. Upon closer investigation, however, it becomes clear that the collage character of the picture prevails. The perspective of the room does not fit that of the table top (or table cloth) in it, and the water jug in its flatness does not correspond to any of the surrounding spaces. Similarly, the facades of the apartment houses in the background seem to be the view through a window, but a closer look reveals that they are nothing but materials which are pasted on the wall. Even in themselves the facades are not a whole section of reality, but a composite of two cut-outs. The whole scene, in other words, is not a unified space, but a composition in which the disintegrating tendencies are at least as strong as the illusion of unity.

What is true for the environment is also true for the portrayed person. The figure of the Engineer is not a whole person, but a composite of a number of heterogeneous elements. The head is a grafitto of what at the time was perceived as the typical physiognomy of a criminal. The body is represented by a machine-age suit which is a mixture of uniform and civilian attire. And the place of the heart is taken by a machine, which appears on the outside of the body as if Heartfield were seen through some kind of X-ray machine.

To realize how different this "portrait" of a person is from traditional pictures, one only has to remember the portraits of such artists as Rembrandt. A portrait by Rembrandt does not only represent a physically intact person, but the features of the human face are unified to a point where almost every detail, every muscle and every shade is shaped in such a way as to express the inner feeling, disposition, and vision of the person portrayed. Grosz' portrait, by contrast, expresses the essential disunity of modern man, and the fateful absence of any inner life. Modern man, according to Grosz, is a clumsy and awkward robot with a machine instead of a heart, the head of an outlaw, and the appearance of an alien functionary. He is a prisoner in a barren cell, and the member of an anonymous mass society. (The facades in the background are pictures of the *"Mietskasernen"* ["rental barracks"] which were typical of the worker's quarters of industrial Berlin.) The inscription on the facade reads: "Welcome in your new home." Considering the abode of Engineer Heartfield, the sarcasm of the inscription is obvious: The environment of the city dweller of the twentieth century is not truly a home anymore, as little as persons are truly human. The world surrounding the modern individual is a man-made wasteland, and the typical being inhabiting it is a caricature of a person.

NOTES ON CHAPTER FOUR

1. Wittgenstein, *Tractatus*, 5.641.
2. Wittgenstein, *Notebooks 1914-1916*, 2.9. 1916.
3. *Ibid.*, 12.10. 1916.
4. Schopenhauer, *The World as Will and Representation*, 1: 5.
5. Wittgenstein, *Tractatus*, 5.632.
6. *Ibid.*, 5.633, (emphasis in the original).
7. Cf. *Ibid.*, 6.373.
8. Wittgenstein, *Notebooks 1914-1916*, 8.7. 1916.
9. *Ibid.*, 13.8. 1916.
10. *Ibid.*, 29.7. 1916.
11. *Ibid.*, 13.8. 1916.
12. Wittgenstein, *Tractatus*, 6.432.
13. Wittgenstein, *Notebooks 1914-1916*, 2.8. 1916.
14. Rene Descartes, *Discourse on Method and the Meditations*, trans.
F.E. Sutcliffe (Hammondsworth, Middlesex: Penguin, 1968), 35.
15. Johann Gottlieb Fichte, "Einige Vorlesungen über die
Bestimmung des Gelehrten" ("The Vocation of the Scholar") in
Ausgewählte Werke in sechs Bänden, vol. 1(Darmstadt: Wissenchatfiche
Buchgesellschaft, 1962), 227, (my translation).
16. Wittgenstein, *Notebooks 1914-1916*, 11.6. 1916.
17. Wittgenstein, *Tractatus*, 5.64.
18. Wittgenstein, *Notebooks 1914-1916*, 8.7. 1916.
19. Emphases in the original.
20. *Ibid.*, 2.9. 1916, (emphases in the original).
21. Wittgenstein, *Tractatus*, 5.61.
22. But to put matters this way is still misleading. For to say that one
has to stay "within" the limits of logic implies that there is an outside.
That, however, is strictly speaking not the case. In the case of the limits
posed by the laws of physics, one can intelligibly speak of going beyond
those limits, for it is clear what an imaginary world is like in which the
laws of physics do not hold. But to go beyond the limits of the basic
laws of logic is unimaginable, one would not know what that would be.
All one would do in trying to transgress logic is produce meaningless
sounds or meaningless marks on paper. This is what Wittgenstein refers
to in section 5.61 of the *Tractatus:*

So we cannot say in logic: "This and this exists in the world, but
not that!"

For that would appear to presuppose that we were excluding
certain possibilities, and this cannot be the case, since it would
require that logic should go beyond the limits of the world; for only
in that way could it view those limits from the other side as well.
We cannot think what we cannot think; so what we cannot think
we cannot *say* either.

The impossibility of violating the laws of logic tempts one to say that
one is, as it were, a prisoner within the confines of logic. But to say so is
senseless, because there is no outside. The limits of logic do not
exclude possibilities (in the way the laws of physics exclude imaginary
possibilities), but impossibilities.

23. Wittgenstein, *Tractatus*, 5.64. See also *Notebooks 1914-1916*,
15.10. 1916.

24. Wittgenstein, "Lecture on Ethics," 6.

25. Wittgenstein, *Tractatus*, 6.432.

26. *Ibid.*

27. *Ibid.*, 6.43.

28. *Ibid.*, 5.632.

29. Cf. Wittgenstein, "Lecture on Ethics," 6.

30. Wittgenstein, *Tractatus*, 6.43.

31. Wittgenstein, *Notebooks 1914-1916*, 30.7. 1916.

32. *Ibid.*, 8.7. 1916.

33. Cf. Chapter I, and *Notebooks 1914-1916*, 7.10. 1916.

34. Wittgenstein, *Notebooks 1914-1916*, 20.10. 1916. The last
sentence of the quotation is a verse from Friedrich Schiller's play
Wallenstein. Schiller is also one of the most influential aestheticians of
German Classicism. In his *On The Aesthetic Education of Man* (1795)
Schiller develops at great length the idea of gaining distance from the
brute facts of life by incorporating them in the harmonious organism of
a classical composition.

35. Wittgenstein, *Notebooks 1914-1916*, 30.7. 1916.

36. *Ibid.*

37. Jean Paul Sartre, "Existentialism is a Humanism," in
Existentialism From Dostoyevsky to Sartre, ed. & trans. Walter
Kaufmann (Cleveland and New York: The World Publishing Company,
1956), 294-95.

38. *Ibid.*, 295.

39. *Ibid.*, 290.

40. Richard Ellmann and Robert O'Clair, eds., *The Norton Anthology
of Modern Poetry* (New York: Norton & Co., 1973), 128.

41. Wittgenstein was familiar with Karl Kraus' periodical *Die Fackel*. Kraus exposed, as much as the official censorship permitted, the ideological and physical brutalities committed in the name of patriotism.

42. Wittgenstein confessed to a colleague in 1920 that he had volunteered in 1914 in order to find death on the battlefield. Cf. K. Wuchterl and A. Hübner, *Ludwig Wittgenstein* (Hamburg: Rowohlt, 1979), 56. Several of Wittgenstein's brothers committed suicide. Wittgenstein himself thought of it on more than one occasion. But direct suicide, according to an entry in the *Notebooks* on 10.1. 1917, he considered, "so to speak, the elementary sin."

43. Cf. Ellmann and O'Clair, *The Norton Anthology of Modern Poetry*, 128. The poem was written in memory of Major Robert Gregory, who was killed in action in 1918.

44. Robert Musil, *Der Mann Ohne Eigenschaften* (Hamburg: Rowohlt, 1952), 18ff, (my translation).

45. Wittgenstein, *Tractatus*, 564.

46. Arthur Rimbaud, *Complete Works*, trans. Paul Schmidt (New York: Harper & Row, 1967), 100.

47. *Ibid.*, 102.

48. *Ibid.*, 104, (all emphases in the original).

49. *Ibid.*, 102.

50. *Ibid.*

51. Arthur Rimbaud, *Oeuvres Completes*, ed. R. de Reneville and J. Mouguet (Paris: Gallimard, 1974), 100-103, (my translation).

52. Rimbaud, *Complete Works*, 101-102.

53. Sigmund Freud, *Civilization and its Discontents*, trans. James Strachey (New York: Norton, 1961), 15. To say that in Freud's thinking, the real self is not the Ego, but the Id, is not to deny that the main thrust of Freud's work was directed toward strengthening the position of the Ego, to increase as much as possible the rule of consciousness and civilization over the forces of irrational nature. Yet, Freud never forgot how precarious this rule was. His description of the conscious mind as the tip of an iceberg shows how much weight he attributed to the unconscious and usually invisible part of the unconscious mind. The pessimism of his later writing (prompted by the manifest barbarism of twentieth century European history) seems to indicate that he did not consider Ego and civilization as the real centers of people's lives.

54. Hermann Broch, *Die Schlafwandler*. Eine Romantrilogie (Zürich: Rhein-Verlag, 1931-32), 20, (my translation. I have also added the sub-title).

CHAPTER FIVE

THE REJECTION
OF TRADITION

THE REJECTION OF TRADITION

"History is an impertinence and an injury . . . Man cannot be happy and strong until he lives with nature in the present, above time."
—Emerson: *Self-Reliance* (*1841*).

"Every situation, every moment is of infinite value, for it is the representative of an entire eternity."
—Goethe: *Conversations with Eckermann* (*1823*).

Wittgenstein aimed at timelessness as a way of life: "If we take eternity to mean not infinite temporal duration but timelessness, then eternal life belongs to those who live in the present."[1] Timelessness is contrasted with endless duration:

> Not only is there no guarantee of the temporal immortality of the human soul, that is to say of its eternal survival after death; but, in any case, this assumption completely fails to accomplish the purpose for which it has always been intended. Or is some riddle solved by my surviving forever? Is not this eternal life itself as much of a riddle as our present life? The solution of the riddle of life in space and time lies *outside* space and time.[2]

The "riddle" of life to which Wittgenstein refers here is the purpose of life,[3] and it has been customary in Christian cultures to consider the acquisition of eternal life as one of the major purposes of life on earth. What is wrong with this idea, according to the *Tractatus,* is the fact that if the gaining of a future life is the purpose of the present one, the same problem of finding a purpose will come up in the future life. For if this life needs a purpose beyond itself to have meaning, why should the next life not need an external purpose as well? The real solution to the "problem of life" is not any goal in the future, but the right way of living now. A person who lives his life in the right way has no need for an external purpose:

> And in this sense Dostoevsky is right when he says that the man who is happy is fulfilling the purpose of existence. Or again we could say that the man is fulfilling the purpose of existence who no longer needs to have any purpose except to live. That is to say, who is content.[4]

We feel that even when all *possible* scientific questions have been answered, the problems of life remain completely untouched. Of course there are then no questions left, and this itself is the answer. The solution of the problem of life is seen in the vanishing of the problem.

(Is not this the reason why those who have found after a long period of doubt that the sense of life became clear to them have then been unable to say what constituted that sense?)[5]

What Wittgenstein is criticizing here is not just a point in traditional Christian theology, but a very basic part of the structure of this life. For the things with which people pass their lives are usually not meaningful or enjoyable in themselves, but only means to gain something else. The better part of one's life, in other words, is sacrificed for the future. Workers do not work because they experience work as fulfilling or meaningful, but in order to gain wages. Students do not study for the pleasure of learning, but in order to gain future diplomas and privileges. The predominant organization of life in Western industrial societies rarely permits the full enjoyment of life in the present, but postpones it, as it were, until after retirement. The basic pattern of Western life involves the constant deferment of gratification; living in the present is replaced by the hope for better times.

Wittgenstein advocates a radical re-orientation, a dissociation from the future which reaches into even the most intimate areas of one's life: "Whoever lives in the present lives without fear and hope."[6] "Fear in the face of death is the best sign of a false, i.e., bad life."[7] People who are preoccupied by future gains or by their death are outside of their selves, they do not exist where they actually are. They fix their attention and energy beyond their real lives, and thus fail to live in the fullest sense of the word. They suffer from a most fundamental kind of self-alienation.

As Wittgenstein criticizes a detrimental preoccupation with the future, he also opposes the corresponding fixation on the past. One of his most extreme expressions of his ahistorical outlook has already been discussed in connection with his solipsism: "What has history to do with me? Mine is the first and only world!"[8] And there is reason to think that his refusal to accept the heritage of his father, to continue the industrial empire which Karl Wittgenstein had founded, to even dress and conduct himself as it would have been expected of a member of his class, or a scholar of his standing in the traditional University of Cambridge, grew out of the same desire to cut himself loose from his past. But the main manifestations of his idea of a timeless existence are to be found in his philosophical works. In fact, his very conception of the nature of philosophy testifies to his determination to live in the present. In section 4.112 of the *Tractatus* Wittgenstein states:

> Philosophy aims at the logical clarification of thoughts. Philosophy is not a body of doctrine, but an activity. A philosophical work consists essentially of elucidations. Philosophy does not result in 'philosophical propositions,' but rather in the clarification of propositions.
> Without philosophy thoughts are, as it were, cloudy and indistinct: its task is to make them clear and to give them sharp boundaries.

By defining philosophy as a process, rather than a product, Wittgenstein ties it to the flux of time. The value of philosophy lies not in accumulated insights which can be inherited from generation to generation, but in the actual exercise of clear thinking. What is important is not the knowledge of the thoughts of past philosophers, but the ability to analyze and clarify any conceptual problem which one might encounter in the present. Philosophers as philosophers have nothing to say, no special knowledge to communicate.[9] Their art is an ability, not any stored information. And its major task is to make itself unnecessary, for where everything is clear no philosophy can exist. Thus one of the major activities of philosophy is to abolish philosophy:

> The correct method in philosophy would really be the following: to say nothing except what can be said, i.e., propositions of natural science— i.e., something that has nothing to do with philosophy—and then, whenever someone else wanted to say something metaphysical, to demonstrate to him that he had failed to give a meaning to certain signs in his propositions. Although it would not be satisfying to the other person—he would not have the feeling that we were teaching him philosophy —*this* method would be the only strictly correct one.[10]

Since traditionally metaphysics was considered the inner core of philosophy, the abolition of philosophy implies the abolition of metaphysical thought. This, in turn, is connected with the impossibility of a transcendent world discussed in Chapter I, and the negating of traditional religious thought eliminates a dimension of the future which coincides with Wittgenstein's idea of timelessness. The abolition of philosophy and the exposure of metaphysics as nonsense, in other words, are but two aspects of the same conception of living "above time."

Another expression of Wittgenstein's fascination with timelessness are his remarks about perceiving things from "the viewpoint of eternity": "The work of art is the object seen *sub specie aeternitatis;* and the good life is the world seen *sub specie aeternitatis.*"[11] Again, the "eternity" referred to is not endless duration, but the elimination of the dimension of time. It has been pointed out earlier that seeing things aesthetically implies seeing them outside of the temporal relations which constitute everyday life and its pragmatic concerns. It can be added that it also implies seeing things outside of their historical context. To see things aesthetically, as art, is to perceive their structure as it exists in one moment. This way of seeing things is opposed to seeing them as phases in historical developments, particularly as links of a chain of causes and effects. To see things aesthetically is to be interested in them for their own sake, to perceive them in isolation from all the other things with which they may be connected. It is to resist the view of things which was cultivated by the nineteenth century with its almost exclusive emphasis on historical and social context.

Wittgenstein's methodological opposition to the historicism of the nineteenth century is explicitly stated in several of his remarks about Frazer's *The Golden Bough,* the short version of which Wittgenstein read at several periods of his life. In these notes Wittgenstein says:

An historical explanation, an explanation as an hypothesis of the development, is only *one* kind of summary of the data—of their synopsis. We can equally well see the data in their relations to one another and make a summary of them in a general picture without putting it in the form of an hypothesis regarding the temporal development.[12]

For us the conception of a perspicuous presentation [a way of setting out the whole field together by making easy the passage from one part of it to another; note by the translators] is fundamental. It indicates the form in which we write of things, the way in which we see things. (A kind of *Weltanschauung* that seems to be typical of our time. Spengler.)[13]

The mentioning of Oswald Spengler in this context is significant, for Spengler was, so to speak, an ahistorical historian. The predominant inclination of nineteenth century philosophers and historians was to see all epochs of human history in some kind of order where one would follow more or less logically from a previous one. In contradistinction to this view, Spengler treated all major known cultures as phenomena which existed in themselves, and which consequently have to be explained solely on their own terms. Spengler's method is thus incompatible with such evolutionary construction of world history as that of Hegel or Marx—thinkers whose incongruence with Wittgenstein's early thinking has been pointed out above.

Out of this frame of reference come certain remarks which Wittgenstein made about the affairs of the time. In a conversation with members of the Vienna Circle he said, for example:

> What should one give the Americans? Perhaps our half-rotten culture? The Americans do not yet have a culture. But they surely have nothing to learn from *us* . . .

> Russia: the passion is promising. Our talking, by contrast, is weak.[14]

The remarks were made in 1931. They express the widespread disillusionment of European intellectuals with their own tradition and the status quo. This was often contrasted with either America as a New World, where a new breed of people would create a new, vigorous culture which was unhampered by the dead weight of the past, or Soviet Russia which in 1917 had succeeded in overthrowing a seemingly invincible and thoroughly ossified social and cultural order. Both alternatives to the European status quo were distinguished by their rejection of tradition as a binding or regulatory force, both seemed to hold the promise of a more authentic life than the "half-rotten" cultural heritage of Europe could offer. It is for this reason that Wittgenstein seriously contemplated emigrating to the Soviet Union to complete the break with his past which in some respects he had already accomplished.[15]

Wittgenstein: Stonborough House

The house which Wittgenstein planned together with his friend Paul Engelmann, and which he built for his sister Margarete Stonborough-Wittgenstein in 1926-28, was conceived in the spirit of the rejection of tradition.

A good deal of Wittgenstein's idea of style is expressed in the way in which in later years he furnished his rooms in Cambridge:

Figure 8. Six views of Interior, Stonborough House

Figure 9.   Exterior, Stonborough House, (1974)

Wittgenstein's rooms in Whewell's Court were austerely furnished. There was no easy chair or reading lamp. There were no ornaments, paintings, or photographs. The walls were bare. In his living room were two canvas chairs and a plain wooden chair, and in his bedroom a canvas cot. An old fashioned iron heating stove was in the center of the living room. There were some flowers in a window box, and one or two flower pots in the room. There was a metal safe in which he kept his manuscripts, and a card table on which he did his writing. The rooms were always scrupulously clean.[16]

Wittgenstein's rooms are functional and uncluttered. Their appeal (and that which would shock more traditional minds) lies in the fact that nothing is admitted which could be considered superfluous or distracting, let alone pretentious or false. Their "austerity" parallels the ahistorical self which sheds everything which is not strictly its own, and which refuses to fill its life with items which are unrelated to its genuine needs. They are a rejection of the stuffy culture which still permeated the life and thinking of Wittgenstein's time, and against which he ultimately directed most of his work.

Wittgenstein's house is internally and externally related to the thought and architecture of Adolf Loos. Loos was Engelmann's teacher, and Engelmann drew the first plans of the house.[17] The similarities between Wittgenstein's house and the private residences built by Loos are obvious, in spite of the dissimilarities which also exist. But most striking is the similarity of the anti-traditionalism which both men practiced. In his famous essay "Ornament and Crime," which he published in 1908, Loos advocated several principles which hold for Wittgenstein's work as well.[18] The following passages are indicative of the style of Loos' architecture:

> I have gained the following insight, and given it to the world: *The evolution of culture is tantamount to the abolition of ornaments from objects of practical use.*[19]

> When I want to eat a cookie then I shall choose one which is plain, and not one which is shaped like a heart, a baby, or a horseman, or one which is totally covered with ornament. The man from the fifteenth century will not understand me. But all modern individuals will.[20]

> The pace of cultural development suffers from the stragglers. I,

perhaps, live in 1908, but my neighbor lives around 1900, and another one in the year 1880. It is a misfortune for a society if the culture of its members is distributed over such a large period of time. The Kalsian peasant lives in the twelfth century. And in [the Emperor's] jubilee parade one could see peoples who would have been considered backward in the early Middle Ages. Fortunate the country that is free of such stragglers and marauders! Fortunate America![21]

We have overcome the ornament, we have reached a state where we don't need it. Behold, the time is coming, fulfillment is near: Soon the streets of the cities will shine like white walls![22]

The architectural context in which both Loos and Wittgenstein worked is well illustrated by the kinds of houses by which the Stonborough residence is surrounded: Most are structurally modern apartment buildings which are decorated, however, by imitation-Renaissance facades, or elements of other style-epochs. They represent the kind of inauthentic mixture against which Loos and his modernist colleagues so violently rebelled: an architecture which tries to disguise factories as Oriental shrines, banks as Greek temples, and railroad stations as medieval castles or Renaissance palaces. Loos and his followers fought not only against the imitative historicism which this architecture practiced,[23] but also against the "modern" Art Nouveau ornaments developed by such Viennese architects as Otto Wagner and Joseph Olbrich. Loos attempted a radical separation of the past by rejecting even the idea of ornamentation, regarding it as inappropriate to an age which built its structures with steel, glass, concrete, and a number of newly invented materials. His idea was to bring the expressions of modern life in line with its actual conditions. And in this, Wittgenstein was in accordance with Loos.

The dominant feature of Wittgenstein's house is indeed that it is without any ornaments—either historical or modern. Its beauty lies in its lack of clutter, and the perfectionist workmanship, which extends from the structure as a whole to such details as radiators, light switches, door handles, and window locks. After its completion, Wittgenstein did not allow the addition of such items as carpets, lampshades, curtains, or any other decorative materials which would disturb the deliberate emptiness of the rooms, and the clarity of the structure and its proportions. The building materials were pointedly modern: The basic materials were artificial stones, metal, and glass. The floors were dark grey, almost black.

The walls were light grey or ochre.[24] Artificial light was provided by two-hundred watt bulbs which shed an even, impersonal light throughout the rooms. The pillars and half-pillars in the halls were shaped like supports which are common "in structural engineering rather than in architectural aesthetics."[25] The whole house is the dwelling of a spirit determined to travel light—to travel without the ballast of accumulated possessions, and without the distracting or falsifying decorations of the past. It is the house of someone determined to live in the present.

Lewis: *Babbitt*

Sinclair Lewis was born in 1885 in Sauk Centre, Minnesota. He graduated from Yale in 1907 and worked as a journalist. In 1914 he published his first novel. His breakthrough as a writer came with *Main Street* in 1920, a novel which implied a double critique of the narrowness and vulgarity of small-town life, and the superciliousness of the pretentious detractors of this kind of life. Lewis' most highly praised and best known novel is *Babbitt,* published in 1922. In 1930 Lewis received the Nobel Prize for Literature. After that his creative powers and fortunes declined. He died near Rome in 1951.

Babbitt is the story of a real estate broker who lives an utterly normal life, and who is constantly haunted by the emptiness and frustrations of that life. He admires those who stand socially above him, and he spends much money and emotional energy to establish personal ties to the upper class—with rather limited success. At the same time he despises and avoids those who are of inferior social standing. He dutifully lives with his wife, although he has fallen out of love with her years ago. (In fact, his marrying her in the first place was more the result of social conformism than real inclination.) He tries "to give the best" to his two children, but he is entirely out of touch with their real needs, interests, and affections. As his business associates, he is a staunch conservative Republican, although that often goes against his conscience and real sympathies. He takes advantage of an established "old boys network" to make good money by fleecing the public, but he resents the coercion which his alliance with the conservative business community creates for his life. Babbitt, in other words, lives what is considered a proper life, but which actually is an existence which is not his own. He lives according to the expectations which others have of him, and thus becomes thoroughly alienated from his real self. Babbitt is a personification of self-alienation. Babbitt has gnawing doubts about his inauthentic life. In spite of his reluctance to acknowledge it, time and again he finds himself wishing for a different kind of existence. The one friend, Paul, to whom he trusts his inner feelings, has similar doubts about the life in which they are both involved. Paul muses:

Take all these fellows we know, the kind right here in the club now, that seem to be perfectly content with their home-life and their businesses, and that boost Zenith and the Chamber of Commerce and holler for a million population. I bet if you could cut into their heads you'd find that one-third of 'em are sure-enough satisfied with their wives and kids and friends and their offices; and one-third feel kind of restless but won't admit it; and one-third are miserable and know it. They hate the whole peppy, boosting, go-ahead game, and they're bored by their wives and think their families are fools—at least when they come to forty or forty-five they're bored—and they hate business and they'd go—Why do you suppose there's so many 'mysterious' suicides? Why do you suppose so many Substantial Citizens jumped right into the war? Think it was all patriotism?"[26]

When confronted with Paul's open criticism, however, Babbitt anxiously tries to deny its validity, and he induces his friend to suppress such threatening rebelliousness. Yet, at one point Babbitt finds that he cannot stand his empty life any longer, and he embarks on an awkward rampage of drinking, adultery, and pleasure-seeking. He even defies the powerful businessmen who try to coerce him into joining a particularly reactionary political action committee. But in the end Babbitt gives up. He resigns himself to living the established roles of businessman, head of the family, and "pillar of the community." He realizes that he does not have the strength to risk his comfortable income, and to set out to look for his own way of life. The only sign of hope which appears at the end of the novel is the defiance of his son who resists the pressure of his father to pursue an established career, and whose self-reliance Babbitt acknowledges as something which he himself should have gained.

It is before this background of self-alienation that Lewis' description of the interior decoration of Babbitt's club has to be seen. This decoration is sumptuous, but it does not have a single genuine element in it. The whole building consists of imitations—eclectic, but tastelessly thrown together by an architect who had to please businessmen with money, but without

any feeling for originality or genuine self-expression. The architecture of
the Athletic Club is as distant from America as the minds of the
businessmen from their real selves. It is an acute expression of
self-alienation:

> The entrance lobby of the Athletic Club was Gothic, the washroom
> Roman Imperial, the lounge Spanish Mission, and the reading-room in
> Chinese Chippendale, but the gem of the club was the dining-room,
> the masterpiece of Ferdinand Reitman, Zenith's busiest architect. It
> was lofty and half-timbered, with Tudor leaded casements, an oriel, a
> somewhat musicianless musicians'-gallery, and tapestries believed to
> illustrate the granting of Magna Charta. The open beams had been
> hand-adzed at Jake Offutt's car-body works, the hinges were of hand-
> wrought iron, the wainscot studded with hand-made wooden pegs, and
> at one end of the room was a heraldic and hooded stone fireplace
> which the club's advertising-pamphlet asserted to be not only larger
> than any of the fireplaces in European castles but of a draught
> incomparably more scientific. It was also much cleaner, as no fire had
> ever been built in it.[27]

Had America realized its promise, it would have avoided the imitation
of Old World styles—imitations which often were imitations of
imitations. It would have renounced the insecure reliance on established
traditions and developed its own style. Instead of prolonging the "half-
rotten culture" of Europe, it would have created a New World. But the
society which Lewis describes was one of fearful, timid individuals who
tried to buttress their feeble selves by slavishly conforming to established
expectations, by acquiring roles and masks behind which they could hide
their impoverished lives. Weak personalities of this kind have a need to
cling to something which seems stronger than themselves. And one of the
things which they desperately try to grasp is tradition. But it is evident
that such grasping is bound to be in vain. Traditions, when they are
genuine, grow out of the genuine needs of those who maintain them.
Once traditions are cherished only because of people's failure to
acknowledge their real situation, former accomplishments are degraded
into disguises which reveal more than hide certain fundamental failures.

Whitman: "O Living Always—Always Dying"

Walt Whitman was born in 1819 on Long Island. He did not receive much formal schooling, learned the printing trade, and afterwards became a journalist. As editor of the *Brooklyn Eagle* he gained considerable recognition.

After Whitman lost his position in 1848 because of his ideological differences with the paper's management, he began to spend most of his time on *Leaves of Grass,* his *magnum opus.* The first edition of these poems appeared in 1855. The book was self-published, and for decades Whitman sold copies from his home. In terms of sales and critical acclaim, *Leaves of Grass* was a resounding failure. Both in content and form the book was far too modern for the average reading audience, and more than a generation ahead of its time. Only a few unusual readers, such as Emerson and Thoreau, praised Whitman for his innovative genius.

From 1862 until 1874, Whitman worked for several government agencies in Washington, D.C. He published several more editions of *Leaves of Grass* himself, adding and changing poems as time went on. In the 1870s, literati in England and Continental Europe discovered Whitman, and he began to gain a reputation in the Old World as an important innovator. In the 1880s he began to be recognized in the United States as well, and *Leaves of Grass* found a publisher and increasing numbers of buyers. Although Whitman never left poverty far behind, he managed to buy a house in Camden, New Jersey, where he died in 1892.

"O Living Always—Always Dying" was first published in the 1860 edition of *Leaves of Grass.*

O LIVING ALWAYS—ALWAYS DYING

O LIVING always—always dying!
O the burials of me, past and present!
O me, while I stride ahead, material, visible,
    imperious as ever!
O me, what I was for years, now dead. (I lament
    not—I am content):
O to disengage myself from those corpses of me,
    which I turn and look at, when I cast them!
To pass on, (O living! always living!) and leave
    the corpses behind!

The poem is modern in its then unusual use of free verse, which implies a rejection of traditional meters and patterns, and the vigorous, almost rude way in which Whitman puts his point. (To refer to former manifestations of his self as "corpses" did not coincide well with the anemic aestheticism which the majority of readers of the time associated with poetry.) And the poem is modern in its expressed attitude toward tradition: It is an unreserved commitment to live in the present, to forego a form of life which defines the self in terms of history or former accomplishments. It thus represents an outlook which at the beginning of the twentieth century became part of the program of such modernist movements as Futurism, Dadaism, or the Bauhaus, that in some cases dramatized their intentions by affecting an inclination to burn down museums and other institutions dedicated to the preservation of the old.[28]

The idea of living in the present itself was not new, although it is an essential component of twentieth century modernism. In 1841 Emerson had published the essay "Self-Reliance" in which he already developed in great detail a conception of self in which the systematic rejection of the past as guide or judge plays a crucial role. On a personal level, this attitude is particularly striking when Emerson defends inconsistency. Noting a tendency among people to be bound by images and postures which they have created of and for themselves in the past, Emerson advocates expressing and stating what one feels and thinks *now,* whether this coincides with one's former self-expressions or not. Emerson thought it important that people have the courage and vitality to contradict themselves, to admit that they may have changed, that they have become someone else. Emerson pleads, in other words, for the recognition of the flux of time, for the temporal dimension of existence. Like Heraclitus at the beginning of Western philosophy he argues against the illusion of fixed, immutable structures or beings.[29] It is this philosophical outlook which Whitman expresses in the above poem.

By expounding this view Whitman evokes a vision of America which had played a significant part in the conception of the United States as the standard bearer of the New World (and which by the time of *Babbitt* had almost become a subversive threat to the reigning conservative mentality): the vision of a republic where people self-confidently relied on their own powers and judgments, instead of timidly seeking shelter in established traditions and social conformity. This vision of self-reliance is well expressed in de Tocqueville's *Democracy in America:*

To evade the bondage of system and habit, of family-maxims, class opinion, and, in some degree, of national prejudices; to accept tradition only as a means of information, and existing facts only as a lesson to be used in doing otherwise and doing better; . . . such are the principle characteristics of what I call the philosophical method of the Americans.[30]

Whitman's poem, in other words, expresses an attitude which has manifestations on a personal, as well as social and cultural level. It indicates a way of life which emphasizes (to use a more recent terminology) process over product, or being over having. And it corresponds entirely to such statements of the *Tractatus* as those in sections 4.112 or 6.4311, where Wittgenstein says that philosophy is an activity, not a body of doctrine, and that only he will live life happily who succeeds in living in the present.

Mann: "Disorder and Early Suffering"

Thomas Mann was born into an old patrician family of Lubeck in 1875. He became one of the most important writers of modern German literature. While his style is seemingly traditional, and patterned after the narrative fiction of the nineteenth century, he developed forms of subtle irony which unmistakably express the non-identification of the writer with his subject matter, and the problematic relation which his protagonists have with their various roles and tasks in life.

At age 25 Mann published his first highly successful novel, *Buddenbrooks* (for which he received the Nobel Prize for Literature in 1929). Among his numerous later works *Death in Venice* (1912) and *The Magic Mountain* (1924) are particularly well known.

After the Nazis came to power, Mann emigrated to Switzerland, and then to the United States, where he lived in Princeton, New Jersey and in Pacific Palisades, California as part of a large community of German emigres. In 1952 he returned to Europe to live in Switzerland. He died in 1955.

The short story "Disorder and Early Suffering" was published in 1925.[31] It does not have much of a plot. It deals with the course of an afternoon and evening in the home of a German history professor, and the thoughts and doubts which the minor events of that day provoke in the professor's mind. The basic topic of the story is conservativism and time.

The story is set during 1923, the height of the post-war inflation which wrecked the German middle class. The value of a dollar was millions of marks. The professor's salary is counted in millions. The thin beer he drinks after his meal costs 800 marks, and after receiving money, the professor's wife has to bike quickly to the next grocery store to buy things before another currency devaluation occurred.

This inflation wrought havoc on the life style to which the professor's family had become accustomed. The family barely hangs on to the house which they inhabit in their upper-income neighborhood, and to the telephone which few of their equals can afford anymore. The house is in poor repair because neither services nor spare parts are available. The formerly elegant rooms are disfigured by woodstoves and pipes. The butler still wears white gloves, but also yellow sandals instead of shoes. Food is poor and scarce. The store sells only so many eggs per household, and the butler as well as the professor's children have to go to the store under assumed names to enlarge their contingent.

Mann uses this situation, and particularly the breakdown of the monetary system, as a symbol for the basic instability of all things, of the inconstant nature of reality. The collapse of the German empire after World War I, and the break-up of the old class structure of German society, are, in this story, a particularly striking example of Heraclitus' metaphysical dictum: "Everything is in constant flux," or "You cannot step into the same river twice."

The break-up of the old class structure is indicated by the fact that the butler and the professor's oldest son are virtually indistinguishable — except that the butler can afford to buy cigarettes. They both dress alike, and the father perceives both of them as "mushiks" or "villa proletarians." (Xavier, the butler, is also described as "a likeable Bolshevik.") The son does not aspire to an elevated social position: he wants to become a dancer, or even a waiter in Cairo. And the butler is somewhat selective with respect to the orders which he chooses to obey.

The professor's children and their guests are casual in their dress, manners, and language. The post-war poverty forces a variety of makeshift attires on them, but they do not mind in the least. They observe or ignore etiquette as they please. And the slang which they use is virtually incomprehensible to their parents. Professor Cornelius graciously goes along with the anarchism of his children's culture, and he does not object to being addressed affectionately as "senior citizen," but in the depth of his soul he feels slightly unsettled. He feels that an order which had dominated European life for a long time, and to which his instinctively conservative nature had become used, has come apart.

Cornelius retires to his study, while his children's party guests arrive. He tries to brace himself for the onslaught of the minor chaos which he expects: the great variety of attire (the sporting outfits and the smoking jackets, the casual clothes next to the gala robes, etc.), the "exotic," mostly American music, the modern dances ("if one can call that sort of thing dancing"), and the fact that girls dance with girls, and boys with boys. The professor's thoughts drift to his own identity as a historian.

Not coincidentally, Cornelius' area of specialty is the Spain of Philip II and the Counter-Reformation. He has profound sympathies for King Philip's attempts to arrest change, to combat the forces of Protestantism, Individualism, the emerging Bourgeoisie, and English Capitalism. Cornelius' sympathies remind him of one of his son's guests, a well-known actor who is famous for his performance of Don Carlos in Schiller's play of the same name. Don Carlos is the rebellious son of Philip, and Cornelius thinks that the actor has a bad influence on his son.

Reflecting further on his self-understanding as an historian he realizes that historians, paradoxically, hate history—namely insofar as history is something which is happening. Historians dislike change, they are attached to what is finished, past, and unchangeable. Actual history is mistrusted by historians as something "impertinent." The real love of historians is directed toward what is dead, ". . . and death is the source of all piety and all inclination to maintain."[32] At the same time, he realizes that there is something contradictory in this attitude, that history is inevitably tied up with change, that everything in history will bring about the forces which eventually will abolish whatever may be.

Cornelius' reflections also touch on his methodological assumptions. When he teaches his students about seventeenth century England, he wants to balance the tendencies of this progressive and rising nation by dwelling on sixteenth century Spain. Cornelius realizes that Spain was doomed, but he thinks that historical objectivity requires sympathy with the vanquished, that a historian must love what he sees cast aside by the inevitability of historical progress. Yet, this very sympathy undermines the objectivity of the historian. Cornelius realizes that as a historian he cannot, after all, stand above the river of time, that inescapably he is tied to the partisan currents of actual historical forces. And this partisanship puts him on the same level as his passionately arguing and demonstrating students. For his students had begun to bring politics—actual history—into the classroom, demolishing the sedate and detached atmosphere which before the war had characterized academic life.

Cornelius continues his melancholy and self-critical thoughts during his customary walk to the mail box. Again, not coincidentally he walks along the river, and he walks upstream. The symbolism of the river in this context is obvious: It refers to Heraclitus' saying that "time is a river which flows endlessly." Cornelius discovers in his thoughts that his life is founded on the impossible assumption that time can be arrested, that the endless river can be replaced by an immutable structure. The faint realization that that cannot be done annoys Cornelius as much as the fact that Xavier, the somewhat insubordinate butler, has a habit of tearing more leaves off the calendar than is called for by any given date.

The one dramatic event of the story is the sudden infatuation of his four year old daughter, his favorite child, with one of the party guests. Cornelius knows that his love for his little daughter is not entirely beyond reproach, that it is tinged with illusion and futility in the way his conservativism is, from which this love originates. "It was his conservative instinct, his sense for the 'eternal,' which has saved itself from the impertinence of time into the love for his little daughter. For a father's love and a little child at a mother's breast—that is timeless and eternal, and therefore very sacred and beautiful. And yet, Cornelius understands darkly that something is not correct and good in his love . . ."[33]

Cornelius feels deeply humiliated, and shaken at the foundations of his existence, when his daughter innocently and unabashedly shows her affection for the young man, crying hopelessly when she has to say good night and go to bed. The harmless event demonstrates to the professor that the time will come when his favorite child will leave him, and when the seemingly timeless family scene will pass away as all things. The innocent suffering of his darling reminds him of the guilt of his conservativism.

The story ends with a comforting visit of the intruding "prince" to the bedside of the little girl, and the father's watching her go to sleep. Cornelius knows that tomorrow the whole encounter will be forgotten, that the usual family scene will be intact again. "How fortunate, he thinks, that Lethe flows into her little soul with every breath; . . ."[34] Lethe is the underworld river from which the shadows of Hades drink, and those souls that are to be reborn and that therefore have to forget. At first the father thinks of what this forgetting will do for the restoration of the idyllic family scene. But then a greater truth dawns on the professor: The child's forgetting will enable her to live according to the Heraclitean Wisdom, namely to live in the present. And in doing so she will avoid the historian's fixation on the past, the piety of death.

NOTES ON CHAPTER FIVE

1. Wittgenstein, *Tractatus,* 6.4311.
2. *Ibid.,* 6.4312.
3. *Ibid.,* 6.5 and 6.521.
4. Wittgenstein, *Notebooks 1914-1916,* 6.7. 1916.
5. Wittgenstein, *Tractatus,* 6.52 and 6.521.
6. Wittgenstein, *Notebooks 1914-1916,* 14.7. 1916.
7. *Ibid.,* 8.7. 1916.
8. *Ibid.,* 2.9. 1916.
9. This seems to contradict the statements which Wittgenstein makes about the nature of reality, facts, substance, etc., and this apparent contradiction puzzles commentators of the *Tractatus* to this day. The contradiction comes to a head in the controversial section 6.54. There is probably no satisfactory way to resolve it.
10. Wittgenstein, *Tractatus,* 6.53.
11. Wittgenstein, *Notebooks 1914-1916,* 7.10. 1916.
12. Ludwig Wittgenstein, "Remarks on Frazer's *Golden Bough",* trans. A.C. Miles and Rush Rhees, in *The Human World* vol. 1, no. 8 (May 1971), 34.
13. *Ibid.,* 35.
14. Waismann, *Wittgenstein und der Wiener Kreis,* 142, (my translation).
15. John Moran, "Wittgenstein and Russia," in *New Left Review* 73 (1974).
16. Malcolm, *Ludwig Wittgenstein. A Memoir,* 25.
17. Leitner, *The Architecture of Ludwig Wittgenstein. A Documentation,* 9.
18. Adolf Loos, "Ornament und Verbrechen," in *Sämtliche Schriften,* vol. 1(Vienna: Herald Verlag, 1961), 276-88.
19. *Ibid.,* 277, (my translation. Emphasis in the original).
20. *Ibid.,* 279-80.
21. *Ibid.,* 280.
22. *Ibid.,* 278.
23. Imitative historicism had already been criticized by the rebellious architects of the previous generation. Cf. the remarks about the "Secession" artists in Jorn K. Bramann and John Moran, "Karl Wittgenstein—Tycoon and Art Patron," *Austrian History Yearbook,* 19-20 (1983-1984).
24. All details stem from Bernhard Leitner's documentation.

25. Leitner, *The Architecture of Ludwig Wittgenstein. A Documentation,* 102.

26. Sinclair Lewis, *Babbitt* (New York: Harcourt, Brace and Co., 1950), 64-65.

27. *Ibid.,* 59.

28. In 1920 the Communists George Grosz and John Heartfield published a manifesto in *Der Gegner* in which they attacked museums and "high" art as useless for the insurgent working class. They expressed the hope that after a victorious revolution the insurgents would create a new culture, one created by themselves. This line of thought was severely criticized on June 9 and 22, 1920 by the *Rote Fahne* (Red Flag), the official paper of the German Communist Party. The majority of Communists felt that the cultural heritage should be preserved and absorbed by the working class, not destroyed.

29. What is maintained by Emerson about individuals, is maintained at almost the same time by Marx about forms of social organization. Cf. Bertold Brecht's "Stories of Mr. Keuner."

30. Alexis de Tocqueville, *Democracy in America,* Part Two, Book I, Chapter 1 ("Philosophical Method of the Americans").

31. Thomas Mann, "Unordnung und Fruhes Leid," in *Sämtliche Erzählungen* (Frankfurt: Fischer, 1966), (my translation).

32. *Ibid.,* 627.

33. *Ibid.,* 650.

34. *Ibid.,* 657.

CHAPTER SIX

THE LIMITS OF
LOGICAL SPACE

THE LIMITS OF LOGICAL SPACE

In section 1.13 of the *Tractatus* Wittgenstein says: "The facts in logical space are the world."[1] And in section 2.11 he says: "A picture presents a situation in logical space, . . ."[2] Thus, facts as well as their pictures are said to exist in "logical space." What does that mean?

Obviously, there is an analogy between "logical space" and ordinary, three-dimensional space: Facts and pictures are in "logical space" in a similar way as spatial objects are in three-dimensional space. But to exist in three-dimensional space does not simply mean to be surrounded by space, but also to exist *as* a spatial object. And to exist as a spatial object means such things as having a certain extension, having a certain location in space, etc. (An object without extension or location, by definition, cannot be a spatial object.) Space, in other words, is part of the *nature* of spatial objects, it defines the kind of thing spatial objects are. That something has a certain height, such and such a volume, and is situated to the left or above certain other things can only be said about spatial objects, and not, for example, about feelings or prime numbers. By the same token, if something is just an inanimate spatial object, then one cannot ascribe to it such things as intentions, religious preferences, or gender. As spatial objects things can be characterized only by space-related features, and space related features can be applied only to spatial objects. If spatial objects are combined with non-spatial features, one gets nonsense like "this piece of wood is irresponsible," and if spatial features are attributed to non-spatial objects, the results are psuedo-sentences like "My thoughts are seven feet tall." To be a spatial object means to be describable in certain ways, and not to be describable in certain other ways. It means to be *limited* in this way.

A special case of the limitations to which spatial objects are subject are the so-called laws of space (the laws of geometry). A spatial object cannot possibly violate the laws of space. A plane triangle, e.g., can have many shapes, and the width of its angles can vary a great deal, but it is impossible for the sum of its angles not to add up to 180 degrees. And a straight pillar in a three-dimensional space can stand in front or in back of a certain area, but not in front *and* in back, as M.C. Escher's lithograph "Belvedere" suggests. Escher's construction represents an absolute impossibility, an object which is literally unthinkable. The architectural design suggested by his lithograph is not the picture of a spatial object, but of something which only looks like one at first sight. It is something which goes beyond the limits of space.

Something analogous to what has been said about spatial objects can also be said about temporal ones. As spatial objects exist in space and are subject to the absolute limits of space, so temporal objects exist in time and are subject to the necessary restrictions of time. Musical compositions, e.g., must have a certain duration, and the basic terms in which they are described are such time-related categories as slow/fast, long/short, early/late, etc. For temporal objects like pieces of music it is essential that their various elements appear before or after one another, and it is as impossible for a composer to put Recapitulation or Coda before the Development as it is for a mathematician to count 1,2,3,4,7,5,6, etc. The limitations of time are as inexorable as those of space.

A further analogy to space can be constructed in the area of colors: Visible objects are in "color-space" as spatial objects are in three-dimensional space or temporal objects in time. As Wittgenstein put it: "A speck in the visual field, though it need not be red, must have some color: it is, so to speak, surrounded by color-space."[3] To imagine a colorless visible spot is impossible. If a spot is visible, it necessarily has *some* coloration, and is thereby subject to the laws and restrictions which govern color phenomena.

It is clear, then, that different kinds of objects are surrounded by different kinds of "space." In Wittgenstein's words: "Everything is, as it were, in a space of possible states of affairs. This space I can imagine empty, but I cannot imagine the thing without the space."[4] It is also clear that these "spaces" constitute the limits of what objects can be. A spatial object like a magnetic field can be large, for example, but it cannot be green, fast, or faithful. A temporal object like an acoustic signal can be long, but not black or tall. And a visible object like hair can be dark, but not slow or infinite. (It is, of course, possible, that an object is both spatial *and* visible, etc. In such cases the object's "space" increases in proportion to the added dimensions.) Its "space," then, is an important part of an object's identity. To know an object implies that one knows its "space." This knowledge is *a priori,* that is, one does not have to find out by empirical observation that a sound is not black, an inflation rate not green, or a piece of wood not irresponsible—as little as one needs observation to know that a bachelor is not married. Thus its "space" is part of the "logic" of an object, or the "space" in question is "logical space." Its "logic" is an integral part of what an object is—that is the meaning of Wittgenstein's insistence that the world is not just the totality of facts, but the totality of "facts in logical space."

It goes without saying that there are other "spaces" besides the three mentioned above. In the analysis of philosophical problems, such "spaces" as the following often become relevant: Emotions (which can be meaningfully ascribed only to sentient beings, but not to such objects as pencils, stones, or prime numbers), moral characteristics (which are applicable to human beings, but hardly to cats, and certainly not to trees or machines), gender (which applies to certain organic creatures, but not to sidereal bodies or cars), legality (which applies in a social or cultural context, but not in the state of nature), and many others. While certain ascriptions are patently absurd, there are many cases where the mis-application of certain categories is subtle enough to befuddle serious thinkers, and where a great deal of conceptual analysis is required to make the violation of "logical space" apparent. Psychologists sometimes describe operations of the mind in terms which apply only to the brain, and sociologists try to analyze social actions in language which belongs properly to zoology or classical mechanics, thereby creating hosts of unnecessary problems.

What holds on the level of objects and facts also holds on the level of language and other media of depiction, for facts and their pictures exist in the same "logical space." Facts are configurations of objects, and pictures are corresponding configurations of pictorial elements.[5] As the configurations of objects are determined by the appropriate "spaces," ultimately the configurations of pictorial elements are determined by the same "spaces." This basically isomorphic relationship is made complicated, however, by the fact that pictures can take a number of forms. That is, one and the same fact can be depicted by a variety of pictures without there being a significant loss. A simple case is given if the form of the picture is essentially identical with the form of the depicted fact: "A picture can depict any reality whose form it has. A spatial picture can depict anything spatial, a colored one anything colored, etc."[6] A map, e.g., can straight-forwardly depict the spatial relationships of a geographical area, a color photograph in a mycology book the visible characteristics of a mushroom, a drum beat (a temporal picture) the pace of a walking person, and so forth. A more complicated case exists when a spatial picture depicts a temporal fact (as in historical charts), or a temporal picture a spatial one (when the position of an enemy is conveyed by drum beats or via Morse code), etc. In this case the form of the picture is not identical with the form of the fact, and yet, the fact is completely depicted. This means that the form of the picture is not limited to the form (the "space") of the fact, but it does not mean that it is not determined by it at all. Not any configuration of pictorial elements is a genuine picture. While a spatial fact need not necessarily be depicted by a spatial picture, the laws of space which govern a spatial fact do place certain limitations on the way in which pictorial elements can be put together, if depiction is the goal.

The way in which the picture of a fact is limited by the "space" of a fact can be illustrated by the two drawings, often called "tuning forks."

The first drawing is a picture of something which could exist; it represents a possible state of affairs. A carpenter, for example, could make such an object. If the object were made, one could say that the elements of the picture are analogous to the corresponding elements of the object, and that the way in which the pieces are conjoined in the picture is the same as the way in which they are put together in reality. Both picture and real object would be within the same "logical space."

The second drawing has no possible counterpart in reality. No craftsman or manufacturer, no matter from however fantastic a science fiction planet, could produce the object suggested by the drawing. The picture represents a logical impossibility. The discrepancy can be pinpointed by marking a spot on the middle "pipe." According to the drawing, this spot seems to be part of the physical object, and at the same time part of the empty space surrounding the object; it would be both empty and not-empty. The picture, in other words, is self-contradictory; it is of the same class of contradictions as the sentence "Smith is a married bachelor."

Since the second drawing presents a configuration of pictorial elements which could not possibly be physically realized, it is strictly speaking not a picture. A genuine picture is, to be sure, not restricted to depicting what actually is the case, but it is restricted to depicting what at least theoretically *could* be the case. A genuine picture, in other words, is limited by the "space" of what it depicts—by the logical limits of what can be the case. It must, as Wittgenstein puts it, be of the same "logical form" as the possible state of affairs which it depicts:

What any picture, of whatever form, must have in common with reality, in order to be able to depict it—correctly or incorrectly—in any way at all, is logical form, i.e., the form of reality.

A picture whose pictorial form is a logical form is called a logical picture.

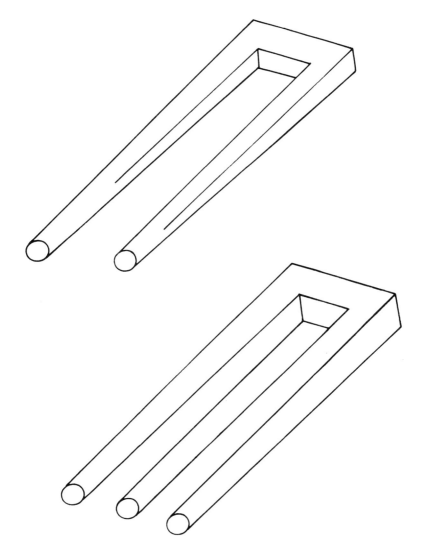

Figure 10. "Tuning Forks"

Every picture is also a logical one. (On the other hand, not every picture is, for example, a spatial one.)[7]

A picture which is not a logical one, i.e., a picture which contradicts logic in a way in which facts cannot, is a pseudo-picture. And a proposition which in this sense fails to be a logical representation of facts is a pseudo-proposition. This is the sense of Wittgenstein's contention that both facts and pictures exist in "logical space," that they are governed by the same laws. By conceiving of "logical space" as the ultimate limit beyond which nothing can go, Wittgenstein found a way in which he could distinguish propositions with sense from propositions which seem to have sense, but which in the end are not true propositions. He could do what he stated as the major task of the *Tractatus,* namely "to draw a limit to thought, or rather—not to thought, but to the expression of thoughts."[8]

Philosophy is, of course, not the only field in which pseudo-propositions occur, but the *Tractatus* mentions philosophy as a particularly fertile field in which sentences without sense are produced in abundance. In section 4.003 Wittgenstein says:

Most of the propositions and questions to be found in philosophical works are not false but nonsensical. Consequently we cannot give any answer to questions of this kind, but can only point out that they are nonsensical. Most of the propositions and questions of philosophers arise from our failure to understand the logic of our language.[9]

Wittgenstein does not work out any examples in the *Tractatus,* but the following case will illustrate what he means (while at the same time providing a parallel in philosophy to the nonsense of the second drawing).

The philosophical idea of "Natural Law" and "Natural Rights" has played an important role not only in philosophy, but also in politics and law. The idea was particularly prominent in seventeenth and eighteenth century thinking, but it has survived in certain forms to this day. Its importance can be indicated by the following consideration. It is a fact of organized societies that certain acts are forbidden by law or custom, and that transgressions will be punished in one way or another. On certain occasions the validity of the law will be challenged, either by challenging individual laws, or by challenging an entire legal system. (The latter will be the case in potentially revolutionary situations, where a whole social order is questioned and threatened.) If a law, which serves as a standard for judging acts, is challenged, then obviously a further standard is needed with the help of which the former standard of actions is evaluated. A law can be judged only by a law of a higher order, and that law, in turn, has to be judged by a law of a still higher order. It is evident that at one point one has to ask what the ultimate standard could be, i.e., what the law of the highest order could be in the light of which all other laws can be evaluated. It is at this point where the notion of a "Natural Law" is introduced. The "Natural Law," since it has to serve as a measure for all other laws, must be beyond the sphere of any actually existing legal system; it must have existed prior to any organized society. It is for this reason that it is called "*Natural* Law," and philosophers such as John Locke have represented it as a law that governs the "State of Nature," i.e., a situation where people have not yet banded together in an organized society with a communal way of life, written laws, police, or government.

The crucial question is whether the idea of a "Natural Law," and "Natural Rights" which are guaranteed by the "Natural Law," is an intelligible idea. How much sense does it make to talk about a "Law" that is nowhere written down, which nobody has decreed, about which no consensus has been reached by people, and which finds no expression in any way of life of a specific community? Is "Natural Law" not a fiction— not only in the sense that something is assumed to have existed in the past which has actually never existed, but further, in the sense that one could not even *imagine* such a thing to have existed? It would obviously be nonsensical to imagine a world where only one person existed, and where this person was a strong competitor. Competition takes at least two. It seems similarly nonsensical to talk about such a solitary individual as having a law and certain rights. Law is something that comes with people interacting with each other, by decree from some authority, or through other measures that involve other persons. And rights, similarly, have to be granted by somebody. The idea of a "*Natural* Law," i.e., a law that could be in the mind of an individual that lives outside of any social organization or tradition, is as unthinkable as a grin without a face. As a grin logically requires a face, so a law logically requires a social context, a context of the kind the "State of Nature" does not provide.

Locke says in his *Second Treatise on Civil Government* that ". . . the law of nature stands as an eternal rule to all men, legislators as well as others." And he describes as the purpose of government the enforcement of this "Natural Law." If a government should fail to do so, or if the government itself violates this "law," then the people have the right and the duty to overthrow this government. (This position has been taken not only by Locke, who was involved in the Glorious Revolution of 1688, but also by Thomas Jefferson in the Declaration of Independence.) But if the "Natural Law" is a philosophical fiction, something like the grin of the Cheshire cat, then the whole philosophical justification of certain political actions collapses, leaving revolutionaries or defenders of certain legal systems with the brute facts of unsupported insurrection or maintenance of the status quo. The decorative cloak of seemingly rational justifications will have vanished, and people will be left with nothing but their passions and their deeds.

The pseudo-concept of "Natural Law" (or "Natural Rights") is one of the philosophical ideas which ventures beyond the limits of "logical space" in the way the architecture of Escher's "Belvedere" or the "tuning fork" does. It is one of the constructions which seems to represent a possible state of affairs, but which actually represents nothing. It illustrates the kind of muddled thinking which, according to Wittgenstein, fills the works of philosophers, and which ought to be cleared out as useless nonsense. And it is the major task of Analytic Philosophy to expose such nonsense for what it is, and to effect this liberating clearing. In doing so, Analytic Philosophy is one of the major means by which the life of the mind becomes uncluttered (in a similar way in which the designs of modern architecture are a means to relieve life of the stuffed interiors and overloaded facades of Victorian buildings). By reducing what is uttered to what can really be said, modern philosophy helps to jettison the ballast which weighs down not only thinking, but all activities of life.

Considering this attitude toward philosophy, the question arises as to what the *Tractatus'* implications for literature and the other arts may be. In his book, Wittgenstein develops a theory of language in which the proposition as a picture of a fact is the model of a communicative expression, and in which logical clarity and soundness is of the highest importance. Since much of traditional philosophy or everyday communication does not come close to meeting the standards established in the *Tractatus,* it may be expected that much of literature or art may have to be discarded as well as unintelligible humbug. That, however, is not the case. Wittgenstein was deeply attached to literature, and he read classical authors more often and more passionately than his Positivistic admirers, or readers in general.[10] In fact, the very theory of language developed in the *Tractatus* which seems so hostile toward everything which is not clear and logically impeccable provides room for the peculiar mode of expression cultivated in artistic works. In section 6.522 Wittgenstein remarks: "There is indeed the unsayable. This *shows* itself; it is the mystical."[11] There are a number of things which are alluded to by the term "the mystical" or "the unsayable," but one of them is what appears in works of art. In a letter of April 9, 1917 to Paul Engelmann, Wittgenstein writes:

> The poem [Graf Eberhards Weissdorn][12] by Uhland is really magnificent. This is how it is: If one does not attempt to say the unsayable, nothing is lost. Rather, the unsayable is—unsayably—*contained* in that which is said.[13]

It is not the factual content of the sentences which make up the poem which is essential, but that which appears by virtue of their order, their combination with each other, their sound, their rhythm, etc. The effect of the poem does not come about by a detached transfer of information, but by evoking an emotional response.

What is decisive for the adequate understanding of the nature of poetry and other art forms is the realization that it is less important whether literary sentences are true or false, logical or illogical, clear or unclear, etc. A logically mangled statement can, under the right circumstances, accomplish perfectly what is to be accomplished by a poem. A poem usually does not attempt to depict a possible state of affairs (although reporting facts *may* be part of the means which a poet employs), and thus should not be judged for doing so either successfully or unsuccessfully. To judge a poem in the way one judges a factual proposition is as inappropriate as judging a screwdriver for being a good or bad chisel, or a bus for being a good or bad boat. A man singing "lalalalala" cannot be reproached for stating things unclearly (because he is not stating anything at all), nor can Gertrude Stein, who, in her 1922 poem "Susie Asado," wrote the following lines:

Sweet sweet sweet sweet sweet tea.
Susie Asado.
Susie Asado which is a told tray sure.
A lean on a shoe this means slips slips hers.
When the animist light grey is clean it is yellow, it
                    is a silver seller.
This is a please this is a please there are the saids to jelly.[14]

In his *Illusion and Reality,* Christopher Caudwell juxtaposes the "rhythmic language" of poetry, and the language of "pure statement of collections of facts uncolored by emotions."[15] He points out that even where statements of fact are involved in poetry, it is not the propositional content which is important, but the emotional powers which come with the more sensual elements of the text:

> We call the primitive's heightened language, which is as if it were speech in ceremonial dress, *poetry,* and we saw how in the course of evolution it became prosaic and branched into history, philosophy, theology, the story and drama.[16]

> The idea of a statement devoid of prejudice and intended only to be the cold vehicle of sheer reality is quite alien to that [primitive] mind. Words represent power, almost magical power, and the cold statement seems to divest them of this power and substitute a mirror-image of external reality.[17]

> Not poetry's abstract statement—its content of facts—but its dynamic role in society—its content of collective emotion —is therefore poetry's truth.[18]

Philosophers try to write propositions, although on a very high level of abstraction, and their ideas purport to represent possible states of affairs. That is why they are a legitimate target for the kind of criticism advocated by the *Tractatus.* Poetry and the other arts, by contrast, may employ propositions and pictures, but their over-all purpose is rarely the mere depiction of possible or actual facts. Inasmuch as the arts do not attempt to depict facts, the *Tractatus'* remarks about logic and language are irrelevant. And this is the major reason why Wittgenstein could be ruthless with respect to the work of his philosophical colleagues and predecessors, while at the same time a connoisseur and supporter of the arts.

There are, however, works of art which fall into the category of propositions, and to which Wittgenstein's remarks concerning "logical space" directly apply. There are, in other words, works which are deliberately and significantly illogical. Examples of these will be discussed in the following sections.

One way of characterizing the specific difference between twentieth century philosophy and earlier schools of thought is by saying that modern Analytic Philosophy insists that propositions can be not only true or false, but also nonsensical. While false propositions can still be credited with having sense, many statements produced by traditional philosophers and other metaphysicians are strictly speaking not even propositions, but nonsense. What Analytic philosophers have discovered, in other words, is the fact that not everything which appears to be communication is indeed that. Consequently, a good deal of what Analytic Philosophy is concerned with is the investigation of the conditions and limits of communication.

Not surprisingly, this is also one of the major themes in the modern arts. In virtually all areas of aesthetic production, "avant-garde" artists have found themselves compelled to speculate about what can be said at all, and to create works which revolve around the idea of an inescapable silence. Wittgenstein's "Whereof one cannot speak, thereof one must be silent" has many parallels in the modern arts.[19] It is in this connection that the frequent and deliberate production of logical incongruities in modern works has to be considered. For illogical constructions are an effective reminder that there are barriers beyond which there is not a new frontier, but nothing. They force on the reader or viewer a kind of self-recognition which will not result in the old pursuit of the new, but in a radical re-orientation which brings into clear view the absolute limits of the human condition. This re-orientation may be effected in serious or humorous ways, and it may result in different practical conclusions for different artists. But in all cases, the encounter with the limits of "logical space" constitute an experience which is peculiar to Modern Art.

Morgenstern: "Sketch for a Tragedy"

Christian Morgenstern was born in Munich in 1871. He was primarily a poet of philosophical ideas, influenced first by Nietzsche, then by Rudolf Steiner. He wrote essays and aphorisms, and he translated Ibsen (whom he knew personally) into German. He is best known, however, for his comic poetry, in which he developed an absurdist kind of humor. Morgenstern died in 1914 in Meran, Austria.

The following poem was published in 1916.[20]

SKETCH FOR A TRAGEDY

A river called Magpie
remembers its true form
and one evening simply
flies away.

A man called Anthony
catches sight of it on his field
and with his shotgun simply
shoots it dead.

The animal called Magpie
too late regrets its selfish act
(for a serious drought simply
occurs.)

The man called Anthony
(and that, alas, is not strange) of
his share of the blame is simply
not aware.

The man called Anthony
(and there's some comfort in that)
like everyone there simply
dies of thirst.

The absurdity of this "Sketch for a Tragedy" lies in its seemingly serious description of a logical impossibility: A river is described as a bird (it can fly), and a bird as a river (it dries up). To describe a river as a bird, or a bird as a river, is not just very fantastic, in the way in which a landscape populated by flying fish or dragons would be fantastic, but the creation of something which cannot be thought or imagined. A river is as incapable of flying as a prime number or a moratorium. The whole subject matter of Morgenstern's poem is literally beyond comprehension.

At first sight the "tragedy" sketched out by the poet looks like a story, and the things mentioned are treated like a story. Upon closer inspection, however, the sentences that make up "Sketch for a Tragedy" do not add up to a narrative, not even a fictional one. It is, to be sure, possible to imagine a river and a Magpie, but to imagine a river that is also a Magpie is more than even the wildest imagination can do. To suggest such a thing is to produce utterances without sense, or "language on a holiday" (to use a formulation of Wittgenstein's later philosophy).

That it is a matter of logic which is dealt with in the "Sketch" is not only indicated by the logical incongruity of the subject itself, but also by the logico-philosophical theory on which the whole "story" is based. The poem states that there is a river which is called "Magpie," and that this river behaves like the bird of that name. The nature of the river, in other words, is to correspond to its name, or the name is to express what the river essentially is. This is part of a theory of language which is discussed at length in one of the most important dialogues of Plato. In this dialogue, Cratylus describes it as follows:

> The use of names, Socrates, as I should imagine, is to inform: the simple truth is, that he who knows names knows also the things which are expressed by them.[21]

Morgenstern makes fun of this theory by dealing with a Magpie River, and by having it behave like a Magpie. The resulting nonsense explodes not only the philosophical theory, but the form of the narrative as well. The reader is left with a text which looks like traditional texts, but which in reality communicates nothing. It is nothing but a mocking refusal to say anything at all.

Rimbaud: "After the Flood"

"After the Flood" is part of the collection of poems called *Illuminations,* which were written in 1872-73. In these poems Rimbaud for the first time makes a complete break with traditional ideas of poetry, producing texts which have all the features of modernistic writing.

"After the Flood" in its entirety is characterized by the disconnectedness of the widely heterogeneous reality fragments which has been discussed earlier. It mixes cityscapes, fairy tales, mythical archetypes, and exotic landscapes, and it produces abrupt clashes of culture and nature, Southern deserts and the Arctic, interiors and geographical areas, etc. But it also introduces sentence and word combinations which gain their shock value by violating the most basic presuppositions of intelligible speech, the laws of logic. The following

excerpt[22] contains several examples of what in Wittgenstein's terminology
are transgressions of the limits of "logical space":

> Madam••• set up a piano in the Alps. The mass and first communions
> were celebrated at the hundred thousand altars of the cathedral.
> The caravans set out, and Hotel Splendid was built in the chaos of
> darkness and ice at the North Pole.
> From then on the moon heard the jackals whine in the deserts of
> thyme, and the pastoral poems in wooden shoes snarl in the orchard.
> Then, in the budding, violet growth, Eucharis told me that it was
> spring.
> Rise, O pond! Foam, roll over bridges and inundate the woods! Black
> drapes and organs, lightning and thunder: rise up and roll! Sadness and
> waters: rise and revive the Great Flood!

The comic effect of "setting up a piano in the Alps" is due to the minor
logical violation involved in substituting a geographical area for a location
in the appropriate sense: "X set up a piano in the Alps" is modeled after
statements like "X set up a piano in the living room." There is a certain
kind of location which is logically appropriate for pianos. These may be
places which are also practically appropriate, such as music rooms,
concert halls, etc., but also locations which would be unusual, such as
garages or blueberry patches. But by substituting a geographical area for a
specific location in this narrower sense, Rimbaud treats "the Alps"
linguistically or logically like "the living room," and that involves
something like the violation of the "logical space" of either "the Alps" or
the location for a piano.

Reference to the "hundred thousand altars of the cathedral" also
involves a logical incongruity, although of a somewhat different kind. Any
building which can conceivably be called a "cathedral" must be within
certain limits as far as size and function are concerned. A church with
100 altars may still be a cathedral, even one with 300 altars. But a
building with 100,000 altars, whatever it is, has become a different kind
of thing, and Rimbaud's use of the word "cathedral" has become a
deliberate misnomer.

But the most clear-cut transgressions of the limits of "logical space" are
given with constructions like "snarling pastoral poems" which "wear
wooden shoes." Poems can snarl as little as pencils can have feelings, or
inflation rates colors. That poems snarl, in other words, is not just
fantastic, but in principle impossible; snarling does not fit into the
"logical space" of a poem.[23]

Further violations of logic are involved in talking about the moon as "hearing," and in assimilating the movement of black drapes, organs, and sadness to the conceptual structure of water. All these constructions are not just bold, in the sense in which the vision of a luxury hotel at the North Pole is bold, but conceptually incongruous. They do not forge unusual visions, but wreak havoc on language, the very medium of vision and imagination. They shock because they make the reader realize that the limits of any communication whatever are being reached.

In Rimbaud's case, the purpose of bringing into view the limits of language and communication is to point to the "unknown."[24] This "unknown" is not a transcendent world, something which could be described in analogy to a region which has not yet been explored.[25] Rather it is a different way of *experiencing* the world, a profoundly wordless way of life. The "unknown" is that which can only be experienced, rather than told or described. It is like that which the Shaman experiences on his "journey," and unlike the dogmas of organized religion. It consists of the visions seen by one's self, rather than the statements handed down from generation to generation by an established church. It is the primary contact with life, rather than the indoctrination with beliefs which are mediated or established by a common language or other forms of social communication. In this respect the "unknown" is like the "mystical" of Wittgenstein's *Tractatus:* it is a "feeling" rather than a describable state of affairs. It is the actual living of something of which attempted descriptions can only be distractions or falsifications.

Marx Brothers: *Duck Soup*

The Marx Brothers were a comedy team that performed with great success on stage, radio, and film during the first half of the twentieth century. There were originally five brothers, all born during the last two decades of the nineteenth century: Chico, Groucho, Gummo, Harpo, and Zeppo. In 1904 they put together a Vaudeville act which by 1917 received top billing. With Gummo dropping out, the rest of the team had its first Broadway show in 1924. During the late twenties they began to produce their first film comedies, usually screen versions of their Broadway plays. Their best known films are: *The Cocoanuts* (1929), *Animal Crackers* (1930), *Monkey Business* (1931), *Duck Soup* (1933), *A Night at the Opera* (1935), *A Day at the Races* (1937), and

Room Service (1938). Their films contain many features in a popular form which later became fashionable among intellectuals in connection with the Theatre of the Absurd.

Duck Soup (Screenplay by Bert Kalmar and Harry Ruby), is a subversive movie in more ways than one. Its plot revolves around the cold and hot war between two fictitious countries, and this situation is used to debunk the pompousness and fanatic seriousness of official politics, diplomacy, nationalism, militarism, secret services, and the kind of posturing which became very acute during the thirties when Fascism was rising in Europe, and when several countries were preparing for wars of aggression. Trentino, the ambassador of the fictitious enemy country, tells Firefly, the leader of Freedonia: "I am willing to do anything to prevent this war." Firefly answers: "It's too late. I've already paid a month's rent on the battlefield."[26] And during the war Firefly tells his compatriot Chicolini: "You're a brave man. Go and break through the lines, and remember, while you are out there risking life and limb, through shot and shell, we'll be in here thinking what a sucker you are!"[27] Political speeches and ceremonies are invariably portrayed as pretentious and hollow, patriotic war declarations are caricatured as a mixture of cheap operetta and religious service, and the usual identification with the "good side" is subverted by the fact that the combatants keep changing their uniforms. Having the same maniacal characters appear as the defenders of the Alamo, Confederate soldiers, or French conscripts of World War I makes hash of the loyalties and orientations which dominated the military establishments and war propaganda of the time.

But *Duck Soup* is subversive not only with respect to particular attitudes and values, but ultimately with respect to everything. The pompousness of official politics and military establishments are not criticized in the name of ideals that are respected or implicitly advocated, but they are subverted in an orgy of total debunking which leaves nothing intact. The film, on one level a farce whose purpose was to provide comic relief during a period of high anxiety, is, on another level, implicitly nihilistic, and the worldview which emerges through the shenanigans of the Marx Brothers is essentially no different from that of T.S. Eliot's *The Waste Land*. The reality of *Duck Soup* is a systematically produced chaos in which the disconnected fragments of speech and purposeful action are kicked around as mere playthings in a game of joyful destruction. The dialogue and acting of the protagonists in *Duck Soup* are methods of making all of reality come apart.

The major means of disassembling the world is the destruction of logic,

Figure 11.   The Four Marx Brothers, from *Duck Soup,* (1933)

i.e., of the structure which underlies both facts and language. By systematically disregarding the laws of "logical space," actions and communication lose their inner coherence, and are thus reduced to nonsense in the strictest sense of the word. This is why punning plays such a dominant role in *Duck Soup* (as well as in other Marx Brothers films). Punning here is not just a means of occasional amusement (as, e.g., in Shakespeare's plays), but the paradigm of *Duck Soup* communication —or rather non-communication. Its ceaseless occurrence is an indication of what has happened to the coherence of speech in the world portrayed in this film.

Firefly: "I danced before Napoleon. No, Napoleon danced before me. In fact, he danced two hundred years before me."[28] In the middle of his speech Firefly changes the meaning of the word "before," substituting the temporal meaning for the spatial one, and thus changing the subject matter of his speech completely. The effect is a comic sort of Cubism, the verbal equivalent of the change of a tablecloth into wallpaper or an abstract form in a painting by Braque. Like Cubism, Marx Brothers puns create a world in which various aspects of reality are forcefully broken up and recombined in ways which destroy any sense of order or orientation: "If you run out of gas, get ethyl. If Ethyl runs out, get Mabel."[29] "This is a gala day for you." "Well, a gal a day is enough for me."[30] Etc. Most of the film's puns are deliberately far-fetched so as to underline the disunity of the fragments of reality which are fused together in them. Ultimately the centrifugal tendencies of the various elements are so strong that the speeches fall literally apart, leaving nothing but disjointed parts without meaning: "I suggest that you give him ten years in Leavenworth, or eleven years in Twelveworth." "I'll tell you what I'll do. I'll take five and ten in Woolworth."[31] In such cases language has obviously ceased to function as a means of communication, its parts do not do what ordinarily they are expected to do. The above utterances are (to use Wittgenstein's expression) "language on a holiday."[32]

The transfer of conceptual confusion from mere speech to action can be seen in encounters like this:

Chicolini: I wouldn't go out there unless I was in one of those big iron things that go up and down like this. What do you call those things?

Firefly: Tanks.

Chicolini: You're welcome![33]

In this dialogue the external similarity of the expressions "Tanks" and "Thanks" serves to eliminate one line of the interchange, thereby exchanging the position of the person who is asking with the one who provides the information: Chicolini and Firefly change their roles. The two speakers, in other words, are *doing* something else at the end of the interchange than what they were doing at its beginning, thereby disrupting the logical flow of the action. And in the following report of a spy mission the logical premises of this action are so badly scrambled that the whole mission becomes unidentifiable:

All right, I tell you. Monday we watch Firefly's house, but he no come out. He wasn't home. Tuesday we go to the ball game, but he fool us. He no show up. Wednesday he go to the ball game, and we fool him. We no show up. Thursday was a double header. Nobody show up. Friday it rained all day. There was no ball game so we stayed home and we listened to it over the radio.[34]

Finally there are what may be described as visual puns. At the end of the war, for example, when Firefly's party is close to being wiped out, the commander-in-chief suddenly shouts: "Help is on the way!" What follows is a parody of the last-minute cavalry rescue known from innumerable Western movies: Two fire engines come racing along, a motorcade of police follows, then a group of marathon runners, sport swimmers, monkeys jumping through trees, leaping porpoises, and a herd of trumpeting elephants. These film clips have no connection with the plot of the film whatsoever, except for the fact that they show objects and creatures in motion. As in the case of the verbal puns, the film fastens on an external similarity to fuse together details of reality which otherwise have absolutely nothing in common, thus creating the chaotic conglomerate of which all of *Duck Soup* is composed.

Duck Soup is a modern comedy in several ways: It creates an utterly fragmented and chaotic world, it thoroughly undermines any kind of traditionalism, it makes such a thing as personal identity (except in a most external sense) impossible, and it celebrates an anarchic irrationalism in the antics of the protagonists. It is most explicitly modern, however, in its systematic disregard for the logic of speech and action, a disregard which renders the whole film into a kind of entertainment in which laughter results from the proximity of total senselessness and non-communication, i.e., from the proximity of total silence.

Escher: "Belvedere"

Maurits Cornelis Escher was born in 1898 in the Dutch province of Friesland. He received his artistic training in the Netherlands, but subsequently spent many years abroad, particularly in Italy. His early work was primarily concerned with landscapes. From 1937 on, however, Escher developed various types of work which deal with such things as optical illusions, mathematical paradoxes, or conceptual puzzles. Escher returned to the Netherlands in 1941, where he lived until his death in 1972.

His lithograph "Belvedere" is from 1958.[35]

The major peculiarity of the "building" constructed by Escher in his lithograph is the fact that four of the pillars connecting the upper and the lower floor seem to be both on the front and back sides of the structure. This spatial impossibility accounts for most of the other logical oddities of "Belvedere." For the ladder, on which two people try to climb upstairs, is at the same time inside and outside of the "building" — something which could not be if the pillars were connected in accordance with the laws of three-dimensional space. And the upper floor, which ought to be positioned exactly above the lower one, seems to be shifted by 90 degrees, thus having the two figures, who ought to look in the same direction, gazing at different parts of the surrounding landscape.[36]

The impossibility expressed in the "building" is represented in condensed form in the cube-like object contemplated by the person sitting in front of the stairway. The decisive feature of this object is, again, the fact that two of its bars are both in front and in back of the construction, thus making it a logical absurdity. This "object," in turn, is modeled after the drawing which lies in front of the puzzled person. In this drawing the spots at which the "object's" incongruities are produced are marked by circles. The drawing, in other words, is the key to the mystery of both the cube-like "object" and the "building" of "Belvedere."[37]

"Belvedere" seemingly depicts an imaginary landscape with a fantastic building. Because of the logical impossibility involved, however, the lithograph cannot be said to depict anything at all, actual or imaginary. Ultimately it is nothing more than a composition of details which are composed in such a way as to render the work a non-picture. It has no relation to any actual or possible world, it does not reach, so to speak, beyond its own limits as an aesthetic composition. It is confined to its

Figure 12.   Maurits Cornelis Escher, *Belvedere,* (1958)

parameters as a work of art. (It is perhaps an allusion to this confinement that the basement of Escher's "building" is built as a prison.) In this respect "Belvedere" is like any of the non-representational compositions by such artists as Wassily Kandinsky. In these "abstract" works, too, lines, surfaces, and colors are not used to depict anything actual or unreal, but to display themselves as merely aesthetic phenomena. They are not pictures, but compositions which exist in themselves and for their own sake. They are "autonomous."

It is with respect to this conscious and radical aesthetic "autonomy" that Escher's lithograph is modern. (His pictorial technique is relatively old-fashioned, which is probably the main reason why his work has never been part of the mainstream of Modern Art.) In its intentional failure to depict, i.e., to communicate anything, "Belvedere" is one of the numerous works of Modern Art which make it a point not to communicate—"to be, and not to say," to use Archibald MacLeish's expression. Relative aesthetic "autonomy" has, to be sure, always been a factor in the art of past epochs. Yet, most texts or pictures of the past did serve such extra-artistic functions as telling stories, glorifying gods or statesmen, reminding people of ultimate concerns and their mortality, and so forth. It was not until the emergence of Modern Art that artists rejected any non-artistic purposes for their works, that rigorous uselessness became a programmatically announced feature of artistic production. It is in the context of this concern with non-communication in which the non-pictoriality of "Belvedere" is significant.

By banning all non-aesthetic purposes from the domain of art, modern artists both reached the extremes of artistic "autonomy" and brought into view the ultimate limits of the purely aesthetic. By creating compositions which in the strictest sense make depiction and communication impossible, Escher represents in "Belvedere" the same extremes and limits. His lithograph demonstrates the absolute limits of communication, and it invites the viewer to contemplate these limits.

NOTES ON CHAPTER SIX

1. Wittgenstein, *Tractatus*, 1.13

2. *Ibid.*, 2.11.

3. *Ibid.*, 2.0131.

4. *Ibid.*, 2.013.

5. *Ibid.*, 2.15 and 2.151.

6. *Ibid.*, 2.171.

7. *Ibid.*, 2.18-2.182.

8. *Ibid.*, Preface by Wittgenstein.

9. *Ibid.*, 4.003.

10. Engelmann, *Ludwig Wittgenstein. Briefe und Begegnungen* 62-73, Cf. the chapter on "Literature, Musik, Film."

11. Wittgenstein, *Tractatus*, 6.522, (translation changed by myself).

12. The poem is reprinted in Engelmann, *Ludwig Wittgenstein. Briefe und Begegnungen,* 63.

13. *Ibid.*, 16-17, (my translation).

14. Gertrude Stein, *Selected Writings,* ed. Carl Van Vechten, (New York: Vintage Books, 1945), 549.

15. Christopher Caudwell, *Illusion and Reality,* (New York: International Publishers, 1937), 25.

16. *Ibid.*, 24.

17. *Ibid.*, 25.

18. *Ibid.*, 30.

19. The poetry of Stephane Mallarmee and Hugo von Hofmannsthal's play *Der Schwierige* are examples of work which deals significantly with the theme of silence.

20. Michael Hamburger, ed. and trans., *German Poetry 1910-1975. An Anthology* (New York: Urizon Books, 1976), 6-7. Because of the poem's presumed allusion to Plato's Theory of Forms, I have used the word "form" in line two, where Hamburger uses "shape."

21. Plato, *Cratylus,* trans. B. Jowett, 435C.

22. Rimbaud, "Apres le Deluge," in *Oeuvres Completes,* 164, (my translation).

23. To say that the sentences in question are not really straight-forward statements, but metaphorical constructions, does not invalidate this observation. The "wooden shoes" of the eclogue may, of course, refer to clumsy meters, and the snarling to the general tone of the poem. But the peculiar force of the metaphor would still lie in its logical distance from the object which it characterizes, particularly

since Rimbaud did not construe the comparison as an obvious metaphor, but in the form of a straight-forward sentence.

24. Cf. Chapter VI, section 3 of this book.

25. Cf. Wittgenstein's critique of metaphysics discussed in Chapter I.

26. Bert Kalmar and Harry Ruby (Screenplay for *Duck Soup*) in *The Four Marx Brothers in Monkey Business and Duck Soup,* (New York: Simon & Schuster, Classic Film Scripts Series, 1972), 143.

27. *Ibid.,* 178.

28. *Ibid.,* 105

29. *Ibid.,* 111.

30. *Ibid.,* 107

31. *Ibid.,* 112

32. See also Wittgenstein, *Tractatus,* 3.322 and 3.323.

33. Kalmar and Ruby (Screenplay for *Duck Soup*) in *The Four Marx Brothers in Monkey Business and Duck Soup.,* 174.

34. *Ibid.,* 117.

35. *The Graphic Work of M.C. Escher,* trans. from the Dutch by J.E. Brigham (New York: Hawthorn Books, 1960), 22.

36. *M.C. Escher: His Life and Complete Graphic Work* (New York: H.N. Abrams, 1962), 154.

37. The drawing itself is, of course, logically impeccable. As the lines of its cube can be seen either as a view of the cube from slightly above *or* below, they do not necessarily involve a contradiction. Only when the vertical lines crossing the circles are made out to be in front *and* in back, as in the cube-like "object," will the logical absurdity occur.

SELECT BIBLIOGRAHPY

Works By Wittgenstein

Notebooks 1914-16. Ed. G.E.M. Anscombe and G.H. von Wright. New York: Barnes & Noble, 1961.

Tractatus Logico-Philosophicus, new English translation by D.F. Pears and B.F. McGuinness. London: Routledge & Kegan Paul, 1961.

"A Lecture on Ethics" (1930). *The Philosophical Review,* 74, (1965).

"Remarks on Frazer's *Golden Bough.*" Trans. J. Beversluis. In *Wittgenstein: Sources and Perspectives,* ed. C.G. Luckhardt. Ithaca, N.Y.: Cornell University Press, 1979.

The Blue and Brown Books. Ed. Rush Rhees. Oxford: Basil Blackwell, 1969.

Remarks on the Foundation of Mathematics (1937-44). Ed. G.H. von Wright, R. Rhees, and G.E.M. Anscombe. Oxford: Basil Blackwell, 1967.

Lectures and Conversations on Aesthetics, Psychology and Religious Belief (1938). Ed. Cyril Barrett. Oxford: Basil Blackwell, 1966.

Philosophical Investigations (1945 and 1949). Trans. G.E.M. Anscombe. New York: Macmillan, 1953.

Zettel (1945-48). Ed. G.E.M. Anscombe and G.H. von Wright. Oxford: Basil Blackwell, 1967.

On Certainty (1950-51). Ed. G.E.M. Anscombe and G.H. von Wright, Oxford: Basil Blackwell, 1969.

Remarks on Colour. Ed. G.E.M. Anscombe; trans. R. McAlister and M. Schattle. Oxford: Basil Blackwell, 1977.

Culture and Value (Vermischte Bemerkungen) (English and German). Ed. G.H. von Wright; trans. P. Winch. Oxford: Basil Blackwell, 1980.

Books On Wittgenstein And On The Modern Arts

Ball, Hugo. *Flight Out of Time: A Dada Diary.* Ed. with an introduction by J. Elderfield; trans. A. Raimes. New York: Viking, 1974.

Bartley, William W. III. *Wittgenstein.* Philadelphia: Lippincott, 1973.

Benn, Gottfried. *Primal Vision: Selected Writings.* Ed. E.B. Ashton. New York: New Directions, 1960.

Bloor, David. *Wittgenstein. A Social Theory of Knowledge.* London: MacMillan Press, 1983.

Bramann, Jorn K. and John Moran. "Karl Wittgenstein—Tycoon and Art Patron," *Austrian History Yearbook,* 19-20 (1983-1984).

Broch, Hermann. *The Sleepwalkers: A Trilogy.* Trans. E. Muir. New York: Pantheon Books, 1947.

Caudwell, Christopher. *Illusion and Reality.* New York: International Publishers, 1947.

Chandler, Raymond. *The Simple Art of Murder.* New York: Ballantine, 1972.

Chipp, Herschel B., ed. *Theories of Modern Art: A Source Book by Artists and Critics.* Berkeley: University of California Press, 1968.

Copplestone, Trewin. *Modern Art Movements.* London, New York: Hamlyn, 1962.

Engelmann, Paul. *Ludwig Wittgenstein: A Memoir and Letters.* Trans. L. Furtmuller. Oxford: Basil Blackwell, 1967.

Fann, Kuang-Ti, ed. *Wittgenstein, The Man and His Philosophy: An Anthology.* New York: Dell, 1967.

———. *Wittgenstein's Conception of Philosophy.* Oxford: Basil Blackwell; Berkeley: University of California Press, 1969.

Freud, Sigmund. *Civilization and its Discontent.* Trans. J. Strachy. New York: Norton, 1961.

Friedrich, Hugo. *The Structure of Modern Poetry: From the Mid-Nineteenth to the Mid-Twentieth Century.* Trans J. Neugroschl. Evanston, Illinois: Northwestern University Press, 1974.

Hamburger, Michael, ed. and trans. *German Poetry 1910-1975: An Anthology.* New York: Urizon Books, 1976.

Hartnack, Justus. *Wittgenstein and Modern Philosophy.* Trans. M. Cranston. New York: Doubleday, 1965.

Hofmannsthal, Hugo von. *Selected Prose.* Trans. M. Hattinger, et. al., with introduction by Hermann Broch. New York: Pantheon Books, 1952.

Janik, Allan and Stephen Toulmin. *Wittgenstein's Vienna.* New York: Simon & Shuster, 1973.

Johnston, William M. *The Austrian Mind: An Intellectual and Social History, 1848-1938.* Berkeley: University of California Press, 1972.

Kandinsky, Wassily. *Concerning the Spiritual in Art.* Trans. T.H. Sadler. New York: Dover, 1977.

Kenny, Anthony. *Wittgenstein.* Hammondsworth: Penguin, 1973.

Leitner, Bernhard. *The Architecture of Ludwig Wittgenstein: A Documentation*. (With excerpts from the family recollections by Hermine Wittgenstein.) Halifax: The Press of the Nova Scotia College of Arts and Design, 1973.

Lewis, Sinclair. *Babbitt*. New York: Harcourt, Brace & Co., 1950.

Malcolm, Norman. *Ludwig Wittgenstein: A Memoir*. Rev. ed. London: Oxford University Press, 1966.

McGuinness, Brian, ed. *Wittgenstein and His Times*. Oxford: Basil Blackwell, 1982.

Moran, John. *Toward the World and Wisdom of Wittgenstein's 'Tractatus.'* The Hague: Mouton, 1973.

———. "Wittgenstein and Russia." *New Left Review* 73 (1974).

Mounce, H.O. *Wittgenstein's "Tractatus": An Introduction*. Oxford: Basil Blackwell, 1981.

Musil, Robert. *The Man Without Qualities*. Trans. E. Wilkins and E. Kaiser. New York: Coward-McCann, 1953.

Rhees, Rush, ed. *Ludwig Wittgenstein: Personal Recollections*. Oxford: Basil Blackwell, 1981.

Rimbaud, Arthur. *Complete Works*. Trans. P. Schmidt. New York: Harper & Row, 1967.

Russell, Bertrand. " The Philosophy of Logical Atomism; Lectures Delivered in London in 1918." *Monist* 28 (October 1918).

Schopenhauer, Arthur. *The World as Will and Representation*. Trans. E.F.J. Paynes. New York: Dover, 1969.

Schorske, Carl E. *Fin-De-Siecle Vienna: Politics and Culture*. New York: Vintage Books, 1981.

Tolstoy, Leo. *A Confession, The Gospel in Brief, and What I Believe*. Trans. A. Maude. London: Oxford University Press, 1967.

Van Peursen, C.A. *Ludwig Wittgenstein: An Introduction to His Philosophy*. New York: Dutton & Co., 1970.

Waldberg, Patrick. *Surrealism*. New York: Oxford University Press, 1965.

Waismann, Friedrich. *Wittgenstein and the Vienna Circle; Recorded Conversations*. Ed. B. McGuinness; trans. J. Schulte and B. McGuiness. Oxford: Basil Blackwell, 1979.

Winch, Peter. *Studies in the Philosophy of Wittgenstein*. New York: Humanities Press, 1969.

Zweig, Stefan. *The World of Yesterday: An Autobiography*. Lincoln: University of Nebraska Press, 1964.

Permissions Acknowledgments

The following illustrations have been reproduced with the kind permission of the individuals, institutions, and firms indicated:

Figure 1: Collection of the Museum of Modern Art, New York (oil on canvas, 53¼" x 25½").

Figure 4: IMP/GEH Still Collection, Rochester, New York.

Figure 5: Collection of The Philadelphia Museum of Art, Philadelphia, Pennsylania (Gouache and Pencil, 7½" x 11¼", A.E. Gallatin Collection).

Figure 6: IMP/GEH Still Collection, Rochester, New York.

Figure 7: Collection of the Museum of Modern Art, New York (watercolor and collage of pasted postcard and halftone, 16½" x 12", Gift of A. Conger Goodyear).

Figure 8: From Bernhard Leitner, *The Architecture of Ludwig Wittgenstein: A Documentation* (The Press of the Nova Scotia College of Arts and Design, Halifax, 1973).

Figure 9: Courtesy of the author.

Figure 11: IMP/GEH Still Collection, Rochester, New York.

Figure 12: Courtesy of Sotheby Parke-Bernet, Agent: Art Resource, New York, New York.

OTHER BOOKS FROM ADLER

SELF—DETERMINATION: An Anthology of Philosophy and Poetry, edited by Jorn K. Bramann. A new, interdisciplinary approach to the modern concept of 'self' through the eyes of the great philosophers, writers and poets of Europe and America, from Descartes to Nietzsche, with powerful new translations.—"An imaginative juxtaposition of philosophers and poets (try to remember the last time you heard Descartes and Goethe, or Hegel and Byron mentioned in the same breath), unearthing long and unjustly overlooked material from Fichte to William Morris to Silesius." **John J. Furlong, Jr.**

$10.95, 256 pp., 8 illus.   ISBN 0-913623-00-8

UNEMPLOYMENT AND SOCIAL VALUES: A Collection of Literary and Philosophical Texts. Issue number 4 of *Nightsun,* interdisciplinary journal of philosophy and literature. As European prime ministers, presidents and labor union leaders wrestle with the concept of a shorter work week and the centenary of the eight-hour work day approaches (May 1, 1986), this timely issue addresses the reduction of labor, environmental destruction and material consumption, as well as self-realization instead of full employment. Poetry by Al MacDougall, Jeff Poniewaz and Antler, short stories by Jochen Ziem and Gerald Haslam, an **interview with Michael Harrington on Leisure and Unemployment** and more.

$6.95, 96 pp., illus.   ISBN 0-913623-02-4

CAPITAL AS POWER: A Concise Summary of the Marxist Analysis of Capitalism, by Jorn K. Bramann. A beginners guide to Capitalism as seen by Marx and Marxists: a clear and concise depiction of the inner logic of Captial and the development of today's society as the logical conclusion of the initial premises of capitalist production. With political cartoons. —". . . a clear and concise overview of Marxist thought and its relevance today. It does not try to persuade, but just to set out in understandable form the basic ideas of Marx and Marxists about the workings of Capitalism and the implications for human life. It should be an antidote both to the distortions of the anti-Marxists and to the jargon of the pro-Marxists, and serve as a sensible grounding for further reading." **Patty Lee Parmelee** —"Capital As Power is nicely compact, has a lot of punch, and should be very useful as a basic statement on the subject." **John E. Elliott**

$5.95, 64 pp., illus.   ISBN 0-913623-04-0

FICTION AND POETRY

THE PEACEABLE KINGDOM, by Peter Wild. A new collection of poems by one of America's most respected poets and 1973 Pulitzer Prize nominee. —"Peter Wild has mastered the art of writing out of a completely personal world while giving the illusion that he is working with and external reality. This wonderful contradiction creates a kind of wholeness of perception that is rare in any poetry." **Diane Wakoski** —"one of the best of the small press books of 1984"**Library Journal**

$6.95, 64 pp., illus.   ISBN 0-913623-01-6

ANOTHER STORY, by Brian Swann. A new novella from a master of the school of experimental fiction. Brimming with realistic details of life in the English countryside and in New York City, a raunchy surrealism invests the protagonist with a kind of purpose as he travels through his time warp, trying to remain sane. —"For Brian Swann, an 'absurdist' writer who actually is one, story comes out of nothing and goes back into nothing. What is left is a residue of voice. Swann's is unique in contemporary fiction: startling, comic, cutting, spare." **Robert Coover** —"Recommended." **Library Journal**

$7.95, 128 pp., illus.   ISBN 0-913623-03-2

UPRISING IN EAST GERMANY And Other Stories, by Jochen Ziem. Translated by Jorn K. Bramann and Jeanette Axelrod. —"Ziem sketches in stark strokes a biting portrait of postwar West Germany in his first collection of stories translated into English . . . As these intensely personal stories unravel, a larger political theorem unfolds: German society is riddled with self-doubt and self-loathing. Ziem suggests that the same wounds exploited by Hitler 45 years ago still fester today . . . (These stories) produce a haunting image of emptiness and despair." **Publishers Weekly** —"Ziem, who moved to West Germany from the GDR in 1955, is a master at exploring the cultural attitudes and assumptions embedded in idiomatic speech. The translations are excellent. Recommended." **Library Journal**

$8.95, 192 pp.   ISBN 0-913623-07-5

ADLER PUBLISHING COMPANY
P.O. Box 9342
Rochester, New York 14604